ESSENTIAL PSYCHOLOGY

General Editor
Peter Herriot

F4

COMMUNITY PSYCHOLOGY

ESSENTIAL

PSYCHOLOGY

COMMUNITY PSYCHOLOGY

M. P. Bender

Methuen

First published in 1976 by Methuen & Co Ltd
11 New Fetter Lane, London EC4P 4EE
© 1976 M. P. Bender
Printed in Great Britain by
Richard Clay (The Chaucer Press), Ltd
Bungay, Suffolk

ISBN (hardback) 0 416 82320 3
ISBN (paperback) 0 416 82330 0

We are grateful to Grant McIntyre of
Open Books Publishing Ltd
for assistance in the preparation of this series

Contents

Acknowledgements

To Boris.

To Marge and Albert.

To Adonis and his sister, Anna Maria.

I am extremely grateful to Alison Cooper, John Rowley, Leopold and Bobby Ullstein for their detailed comments; and of course, to the people I interviewed. I should also like to thank Ken Boyce, Stewart Marks and Nigel Armistead for their comments on certain sections.

Editor's Introduction

Mike Bender doesn't want community psychology to become another -ology or -ism. So instead of presenting it as a neat, applied psychology 'package', he discusses how and why it has developed, and describes what some individuals are doing now in the way of community psychology. Ranging from a local authority educational psychology service to the Islington Bus Company, he shows how the community psychologist cannot see the individual as an isolated case. Rather, he has to become familiar with and utilize all the resources available to him in the community, whether statutory or voluntary, formal or informal. He concludes with a plea for changes in the training of psychologists, but insists that in the end 'What a psychologist does depends on his priorities, his values.'

Community Psychology belongs to Unit F of *Essential Psychology*. What unifies the books in this unit is the concept of change, not only in people but also in psychology. Both the theory and the practice of the subject are changing fast. The assumptions underlying the different theoretical frameworks are being revealed and questioned. New basic assumptions are being advocated and consequently new frameworks constructed. One example is the theoretical framework of 'mental illness': the assumptions of normality and abnormality are being questioned, together with the notions of 'the cause', 'the cure', and 'the doctor-patient relationship'. As a result, different frameworks are developing, and different professional practices gradually being initiated. There are, though, various social and political structures which tend to inhibit the translation of changing theory into changing practice.

One interesting change is the current aversion to theoretical frameworks which liken human beings to something else. For example, among many psychologists the analogy of the human being as a computer which characterizes Unit A is in less favour than the concepts of development (Unit C) and the person (Unit D).

Essential Psychology as a whole is designed to reflect this changing structure and function of psychology. The authors are both academics and professionals, and their aim has been to introduce the most important concepts in their areas to beginning students. They have tried to do so clearly, but have not attempted to conceal the fact that concepts that now appear central to their work may soon be peripheral. In other words, they have presented psychology as a developing set of views of man, not as a body of received truth. Readers are not intended to study the whole series in order to 'master the basics'. Rather, since different people may wish to use different theoretical frameworks for their own purposes, the series has been designed so that each title stands on its own. But it is possible that if the reader has read no psychology before, he will enjoy individual books more if he has read the introductions (A1, B1 etc.) to the units to which they belong. Readers of the units concerned with applications of psychology (E, F) may benefit from reading all the introductions.

A word about references in the text to the work of other writers – e.g. 'Smith (1974)'. These occur where the author feels he must acknowledge an important concept or some crucial evidence by name. The book or article referred to will be listed in the References (which double as Name Index) at the back of the book. The reader is invited to consult these sources if he wishes to explore topics further. A list of general Further Reading is also to be found at the back of this book.

We hope you enjoy psychology.

Peter Herriot

I
The development of community psychology

What is this thing called 'community psychology'?

'Community psychology' as a formal theory or discipline does not exist in Britain. Hopefully, it never will. For if it did, it would join the large numbers of sadly withering 'isms' and 'ologies' that proliferate in psychology. Thus, the purpose of this book is not to propound yet another approach purporting to have an answer. Rather, it will outline certain areas that applied psychologists have neglected or ignored and which seem worth further exploration. To the extent that 'community psychology' has any coherence, it is as a reaction against mainstream attitudes and practices in applied psychology, and is an attempt to improve them. It is asking: what should applied psychologists be doing to alleviate unnecessary psychic distress; what can they do to make psychology relevant to problems facing people today?

Plan of the book
After outlining what 'community psychology' is, I describe its historical antecedents and the attributes and attitudes that seem to characterize its various endeavours. These sections rely heavily on American work, as psychology, especially applied psychology in the community, is effectively an American development. However, in the second part of the book, I give examples of British work which illustrate the various themes of community psychology, and where possible I have used inter-

views in order to give the feel of applied work. The book concludes with a section on research and training and possible future developments.

The ingredients

Community psychology is an attempt to fuse two traditions, the psychological and the sociological/political. Since they have different philosophical bases, and since community psychologists tend to fall into one camp or the other, trying to provide an overarching definition of community psychology is not easy. Perhaps we can best start by looking at the connotations of the two words in the term.

Psychology, like economics, anthropology, and sociology, is one of the social sciences. Greenstein, in Lipset (1969), points out one characteristic that distinguishes it from the latter two – its emphasis on intrapsychic causality:

> Psychology like sociology evidently aspires to advance general propositions about behaviour . . . psychology deals with the personal system, sociology with the social system . . . psychology is concerned with those determinants of behaviour that arise from within individuals, sociology with the effects of the environment . . . on individuals' behaviour.

A second important difference is that psychologists, compared with other social scientists, attach more importance to the experimental method, and are more sceptical of observational studies. Often this results in trivia, but it does have the merit that if another psychologist repeats an experiment on a population similar to that of the original study and fails to replicate its results, the conclusions of the original study lose some of their plausibility. The experimental method provides a neutral testing ground for differences of opinion and allows a body of knowledge to be developed.

These two qualities define, then, the usefulness of the psychologist to society. He has a specialist knowledge about individuals and their development; and a method of testing his ideas so that they do not just depend on his say-so. However, if psychology is essentially about predicting what people will do by means of studying them as individuals and in a way amenable to experimental design, then obversely, one of its limitations is that it is not going to have much to say about the society in which these individuals find themselves (see B5);

10

and this is especially so if societal variables are far more difficult to specify than individual ones and less amenable to studying in the laboratory. Quite a few psychologists now feel that their subject should have more to say about persons-in-societies and have become interested in utilizing more sociological and organizational concepts in their thinking.

Community: There are over a hundred definitions of this term (Bennington in Jones and Mayo, 1974). It can mean such diverse things as a group of scholars ('the scientific community'), ethnic groups ('the Irish community'), neighbourhoods ('the community of Stepney'). Generally, however, community studies tend to have concentrated on working-class localities. Jackson (1968) suggests that the middle-class periodically re-discover and re-analyse the rough charms of the masses, and that the present interest stems from and was shaped by the work of the Institute of Community Studies, which was founded by Michael Young and Peter Wilmott, and can be dated from their book '*Family and Kinship in East London*' (1957). This was a report of a rather poorly carried out survey of people living in Bethnal Green. It was very influential, partly because it was readable – a great rarity among social science literature – and also because it was part of the groundswell of the late 'fifties. After the uniformity, stability, and drabness of the post-war years, there was a demand for a more colourful and active society. And where does one find colour and activity? Why, down the Old Kent Road and even more up North, whose grimy charms were celebrated in a host of bestsellers – Braine's *Room at the Top*, Sillitoe's *Saturday Night and Sunday Morning*, Storey's *This Sporting Life*, Barstow's *A Kind of Loving*, etc.

Perhaps we can best understand the emotional appeal of community studies by quoting from a sociologist of the same school, Brian Jackson (1968:15). He gives Lowry as an example of an artist whose work embodies the working-class experience:

> But they remain very lonely paintings ... With Lowry it is as if the painting is a window view of life: the life is 'out there' but you are separate from it. No working-class artist could have created them: to be so clear-sighted, or so self-conscious, about 'community' one has to be outside it and living a life of individual realisation that the packed, public sociability of the working-class denies. Nevertheless that life of 'individual real-

11

isation' desires what, in the given situation, it cannot have—those very capacities for dense mutuality which would cramp it. The working-class debate, or rather the relationship between the debators and their subject is trapped there forever.

Jackson highlights well a tension in many leftwing novelists, e.g. Orwell, and social scientists: the attempt to retain their identity and at the same time fuse it in a strongly knit group.

This tension is of importance in understanding the motivation of community psychologists, because community psychology can usefully be seen as an attempt to resolve it. If by their efforts and skills, the psychologists could somehow raise the consciousness of the working class (see B5), help them to tackle and solve the problems pressing in on them, they would be sharing a similar world-view; and the kind of communication that the psychologists are accustomed to with other middle-class intellectuals would be possible. This goal is of course illusory. If we follow the work of Bernstein (1973), (see C2), a group's language and its forms are an integral part of its experience, and thus if we change the language and thought-paths, we radically change that group's cultural ways. Once a person steps back from his absorbing identity as a group member and questions the motives of his actions, the smooth unfolding of behaviour and the predictability of the other members of the group both decrease, and we have a quite different small group system (see B2).

Thus, besides providing a rather dubious emotional underpinning to community psychology, the attempt to resolve this tension between self-consciousness and belonging has been a factor in shaping its goals. For it is a striking fact that community psychology, along with community social work and community psychiatry, is nearly exclusively concerned with the 'inner city' areas, as American sociologists like to refer to the high-density, poor housing, multi-racial central areas of the large cities. Although translated into the more neutral social science language of mental illness, deviancy, alienation, delinquency, etc. (see F8), part of the driving force behind community psychology work is the desire actively to help the underprivileged and deprived.

The latter are naturally overrepresented in 'the inner-city' areas, and are very inadequately reached by the existing statutory services (cf., e.g., Hollingshead and Redlich, 1958; Sarason *et al.*, 1966; 1967). Thus, having decided to work in such areas, community psychologists had to work out new methods of attracting and reaching the clients. For example, Sarason *et al.* noted that the high drop-out rate from child guidance clinics in New Haven was partly due to the clinics requiring that the mother bring the child. Since, in a poor area with a high proportion of single parent families, the mother was often working, this meant that only the better off and most highly motivated mothers would attend. (Functionally, the requirement served a useful purpose for the clinic, as it prevented many of the most intractable cases reaching the clinic. Note that this requirement was justified as good professional practice. For the clinic workers to say that they actually did not want to see such cases would be to accuse themselves of professional irresponsibility.) Sarason and his colleagues arranged to chauffeur children to the clinic, which cut the drop-out rate to near zero.

Community psychology

There are a great variety of approaches subsumed under the term 'community psychology' and thus the utility of a general definition is dubious. I would define it as 'attempts to make the fields of applied psychology more effective in the delivery of their services, and more responsive to the needs and wants of the communities they are serving.' Scribner (in Cook, 1970) defines it as 'at the present time a convenient umbrella term for psychologists who share a concern for a large role for psychology on the social problems of the day but who have varying ideologies, values, psychological orientations and knowledge, skills and techniques.'

Both these definitions imply something further – a dissatisfaction with the way psychological services are currently being administered. Thus, optimistically, community psychology is part of the vanguard of applied psychology and its essence is a *reaction* against traditional approaches. So we must look at what it is reacting against. The next section traces the postwar history of applied psychology that led up to the development of 'community psychology' (see too F3).

Developments in the treatment of the mentally ill and handicapped, 1945–65

Applied psychology

A psychology graduate who wishes to stay in the field has two main options: the academic field (teaching and research), and the applied fields. The three main applied fields are educational, clinical, and industrial/occupational. The last is not usually associated with community psychology, and indeed I know little about it (see Unit E). For recognition as an educational psychologist in England and Wales, a minimum of another four years' work is needed. One must gain a teaching diploma, teach for two years, and then pass a course in educational psychology. (In Scotland, an honours degree and teaching experience is often sufficient.) There are two paths to becoming a clinical psychologist (see F3). One can either take a two year postgraduate course or one can become a probationary psychologist in the NHS, work in a variety of hospitals, and at the end of three years, seek accreditation from the British Psychological Society.

Educational psychology

The first educational psychologist, Cyril Burt, was appointed by the London County Council in 1913, but there were only a handful until after World War II. Many psychologists worked for the armed services during the war and their work made the utility of applied psychology visible to a much wider range of potential employers. By the mid-fifties, the profession was well-established. There were 324 educational psychologists in England and Wales in 1964, and by 1974 the number had doubled to 638. They work with children having learning and/or emotional difficulties, either in schools or child guidance clinics. Their status is probably higher than that of clinical psychologists, perhaps because they are better known to the public, and also because they have a statutory role – a child can only be deemed 'educationally subnormal' after a psychologist's assessment (see F2). However, their contribution to preventive work is limited by the large number of assessments they do.

Clinical psychology

In this book, we shall be most concerned with progress and change in clinical psychology. Initially, the main *raison d'être* of clinical psychologists was assessments (see F3). The psychotropic drugs (see below) have different effects on different types of mental illness, and thus the correct diagnosis became a matter of some importance. Psychiatrists, as the heads of mental hospitals, created posts for psychologists, so that the latter could see patients, and on the basis of their interview and tests, give an opinion as to diagnosis. To this rather limited role, psychologists often added therapy. In the postwar years, this would usually have been psychodynamic – since behaviour therapy had not been invented – so psychoanalysis was still the main therapeutic school (see F3). A similar pattern of skills developed in America where clinical psychology expanded rapidly after the war, mainly because of the needs of the Veterans' Administration. This organization was responsible for the rehabilitation and care of the many ex-soldiers who had become mentally ill during the war. Extremely well financed, it hired a great number of psychologists and encouraged the setting up of many training courses (Shakow, 1969).

In 1968, there were some 500 active clinical psychologists in Britain. Like educational psychology, the profession became established and expanded after 1945. Most clinicals work in the NHS, mainly in psychiatric and subnormality hospitals. While psychologists assess and treat patients, these patients remain the responsibility of doctors, nearly always psychiatrists. Thus, at present all patients being treated by a clinical psychologist need medical cover, a source of some contention. The situation may be changed when the Trethowan Committee reports. Psychologists also usually do some teaching, mainly to nurses. Some also carry out research, but probably the majority of that is done full-time in Medical Research Council Units or teaching hospitals.

Changes in psychiatry

Before proceeding, two points are in order. First, I shall frequently be referring to 'mentally ill' persons. By this, I mean persons who have emotional difficulties affecting their own or others' lives detrimentally. I am making no statement as to the cause of these difficulties, except that it is clear that they are not suffering from any illness (see F1). *Psychic distress cannot be*

15

equated with a physical illness. Even what is considered the most severe mental illness, schizophrenia, has not been shown to have a physical or organic basis (Rosenthal and Kety, 1968). However, while not liking the term 'mental illness', I shall not substitute for it terms like 'problems of living' (Szasz, 1962) or 'personal distress' (Foulds, 1965) which, while having different connotations, are roughly its equivalent.

Second, as already mentioned, the number of psychologists has jumped in recent years, and the number of psychiatrists has also greatly increased. This might give the impression that more and more people are cracking up. Arthur (1971) has reviewed the evidence, and has shown that this is not the case for the psychoses. For a given culture, the rate of admission seems to have been remarkably consistent across time. The issue is complicated by the fact that probably only a minority of persons with emotional difficulties seek professional help. Also, seeing a psychiatrist is much easier and less stigmatizing than it was previously. Thus, it is difficult to know whether more people need mental health services than previously, or whether the same percentage of the population has always needed them, but is now more willing to seek them.

Mental hospitals were previously asylums for the insane or colonies for subnormals, often built in Victorian times. The city fathers bought land well away from the city, partly because they thought mental illness was contagious, like cholera; partly because they believed, not without evidence (Grob, 1966), that calm and countryside would be beneficial to the afflicted; and, we may suspect, because they wanted to be rid of an unpredictable and 'difficult' sector of the population. For London, the main groupings are around Watford to the north-west, and Epsom to the south. (If you're going through by train, you can recognize them by their boiler-house chimneys.) These hospitals developed out-patient facilities in their catchment areas, but if a person needs in-patient treatment, he has to travel to the main hospital. Thus, for example, a resident of the London borough of Newham can quite easily see a psychiatrist on an out-patient basis but if he needs in-patient treatment when mentally ill, he will have to travel eight miles to Goodmayes, and if mentally handicapped, over twenty miles to South Ockendon. It is ironic that it is far easier to see a psychiatrist on an out-patient basis than a psychologist. Although the latter criticize the former for considering mental illness to be an intrapsychic, if not an organic phenomenon, and for underestimating familial and environmental variables, it is the psychologists who have shown far greater reluctance to move out of their institutions, and thus most work outside the cities whose populations they serve.

The main accommodation for the mentally ill remains, then, the mental hospital, with anything up to 2,000 beds. Recently, a number of district general hospitals have been built in the catchment areas and include a psychiatric, and sometimes a subnormality, wing. Due to the very high cost of city land, progress has been slow, but some psychologists are now working in these new hospitals.

Since the early fifties, there have been two major changes in the way mental hospitals function. The first was *the unlocking of the wards*. Before the war, mental illness was considered a function of the personality and thus a permanent condition. There were strong connotations of violence, although in fact the crime rate of mental patients is lower than that of 'normals'. Thus, a prewar superintendent of an Essex mental hospital boasted that no one diagnosed as schizophrenic ever left his hospital again. After the war, psychiatrists came to notice that locking wards promoted regression, apathy, and institutionalization, so that patients after a couple of years were very often unable to function outside the hospital environment (Wing and Brown, 1970). The opening of wards indicated a change of approach – patients should and could be returned home as soon as possible. If the main reason for a person being in a mental hospital is that he is showing symptoms of mental illness, it often happens that in the new (hospital) environment, these remit. So he becomes no longer mentally ill and can be discharged. (He may still not be functioning at a high level, but 'functioning' is not a medical concept, but a societal one, and thus should not in itself determine hospitalization.) (Foulds, 1965.)

At the same time, the medical model of mental illness was losing ground. While the research evidence suggests that the psychoses have a genetic component, the inability of medical research workers, after spending very large sums of money, to show any biochemical dysfunction in 'diseases' like manic depression or schizophrenia, gradually eroded the credibility of the model. Its alternative – the view that mental illness was a result of environmental stress and thus reversible, correspond-

17

ingly gained ground. This change of attitude can in part be attributed to Maxwell Jones, a psychiatrist who worked at the Henderson Hispital, Surrey, and then at Dingleton, Morayshire, and who turned these hospitals into 'therapeutic communities' (cf. his *Social Psychiatry*, 1962). He tried to minimize the role distance between nurses and patients, so that they could communicate on a more equal, less dehumanizing basis, and to create powerful group pressures towards achieving greater insight and functioning. To this end, the patients attended a very large number of groups – meetings of the whole ward, therapeutic groups, etc. Decisions, such as whether a person should be admitted to the hospital, were made by the patients as well as by the professional workers. While few hospitals have followed Jones in converting themselves into therapeutic communities (but see Martin, 1962, for the Claybury experience) quite a few have a single ward – usually the admission ward for neurotics – where this approach is practised. Overall, Jones's ideas, which were a long way ahead of their time, had a tremendous influence by suggesting that the patient could be actively helped to help himself, needn't spend his days in hospital, and that the traditional mental nurse–patient relationship was psychonoxious. (cf. Caine and Smail, 1969.)

The second major change occurred at around the same time. This was *the introduction of psychotropic drugs*. Before then, there were no drugs that actually diminished symptoms of mental illness. The first drug that was able to do this was Chlorpromazine ('Largactil') which was strikingly successful in reducing schizophrenic symptoms, and is still after twenty years the market leader. It was the first of the 'major tranquillizers'. (The minor tranquillizers, such as Valium and Librium, are used for neurotic anxiety states.) The schizophrenic was and is by far the greatest user of mental hospitals (44 per cent of all in-patients in 1971) and tended to stay in them without being discharged, thus becoming 'chronic', i.e. very difficult to help. With the introduction of the major tranquillizers, it was possible to diminish the active symptoms that had brought them into hospital, and when the most suitable drug, and its dosage, had been ascertained, they could be discharged with arrangements for them to continue receiving their pills (and more recently, long-lasting injections) from their GPs or out-patient psychiatric clinics. (As an aside, it is probably worth mentioning that it is fallacious to think that the psychotropic drugs are merely sedatives. Obviously, at very high dosages they are, but their effects are both more specific and more complex than mere sedation (Stevens, 1973). In the field of psychogeriatrics, their effect in removing mental illness can be remarkable.)

The advent of psychotropic drugs seemed to herald a new era in mental health practice. The custodial era was passing and these drugs would allow the client, previously absorbed in his fears and anxieties, to communicate. Through therapy, their level of insight and functioning would increase so that they would be able to cope with environmental stresses.

Unfortunately, things didn't work like that. On the one hand, psychiatrists were ill-trained to conduct therapy. Instead, their work came to consist mainly of prescribing drugs and monitoring their effects. On the other, those psychiatrists and psychologists who were interested in therapy, couldn't deliver the goods. Their therapy was geared to high verbal and abstract ability, and even when not distracted by their symptoms, psychotics aren't very good in these abilities. So what happened was that the number of long-stay patients decreased. (The number of resident patients decreased by 28 per cent between 1954 and 1971.) The average stay per patient went down radically. In one Essex hospital, thirty days is now the average length of stay and this is by no means atypical. However, the patient still fails to live at a higher level of functioning. Studies consistently show that 30–40 per cent of patients will be back in hospital within six months, and 65–75 per cent within three to five years. At best, only 50 per cent will be working (Anthony et al., 1972). Faced with difficulties after discharge – often discharged to the family situation which had caused the initial breakdown – the patient is still unable to cope. The back ward chronic had been replaced by the revolving door chronic. However, this has meant that fewer beds are needed, and so there is less overcrowding on the wards.

The psychotropic drugs have one unambiguously beneficial effect. The physical treatments – leucotomies, insulin comas, and to a lesser extent electroconvulsive therapy – became less fashionable. Since a leucotomy severs one part of the brain from the rest and thus is irreversible, this decrease in barbarity was welcome (see F8).

Summarizing then, the main developments in mental hospital treatment since the war have been the unlocking of wards, the introduction of psychotropic drugs, a decrease in the number of beds due to the decrease in length of stay per patient and the advent of the 'revolving door chronic', and the decrease in the use of physical methods. (See also pp. 24–5).

Changes in the role of the clinical psychologist

As already mentioned, the main functions of the clinical psychologist were and are psychotherapy and assessment. Already by the end of the fifties, these had been seriously discredited.

Considering therapy first, data were produced showing that individual psychotherapy was no more effective than leaving the client alone to get better ('spontaneous remission'). The key evidence is that of Eysenck (1952) on the treatment of adults, and Levitt (1957) on that for children. Although one may be sceptical as to what 'spontaneous remission' might mean, and of the validity of lumping a large number of studies together, these articles attracted tremendous attention. They suggested that mental health professionals had grossly oversold their utility, and that the assumption that people with problems should seek professional help might be false. For example, Shepherd *et al.* (1971), in a study in Buckinghamshire, found that for every child referred to a child guidance clinic, there was another with very similar problems that wasn't, and the key variable determining referral turned out to be maternal anxiety. In the follow-up, it was found that the rate of symptom improvement was about the same, whether the child was treated or not.

Truax and Carkhuff (1967) were later to show that what was happening was that some therapists achieve high rates of success, whilst others are so unempathic and cold that they're psychonoxious – their attempts at therapy actually make the client worse. That was ahead. At the time, Eysenck's writings had the important effect of discrediting psychoanalysis, the main form of therapy available. Defenders, like Storr (in Rycroft, 1966) could write that the aim of psychoanalysis was not to 'cure' patients; rather it was to increase self-understanding. However, this was hardly reassuring as he also quotes London (1964) that 'the American Psychoanalytic Association ... undertook a survey to test the efficacy of psychoanalysis. The results were so disappointing that they were withheld from publication.'

The loss of prestige suffered by psychoanalysis, which was

perhaps greater in this country than in America where it was strongly entrenched in the medical schools, had a liberating effect on psychological theorizing. Psychoanalysis, with its central tenet of man as the slave of his instincts, is culturally ignorant and has nothing to say about the social determinants of mental illness (see F1). It has very little to offer the psychotic (as Freud recognized) and less verbally able. Thus, its range of utility is very limited.

The more hardheaded clinical psychologist who scorned psychoanalysis preferred to see himself as an assessor of personality and its disorders, using scientifically validated measures. However, surveys by Meehl (1954) and Ellis (1953) showed very poor validity for personality and clinical tests.

The whole role model of the psychologist as therapist and assessor was shown to have dubious utility by a study of manpower needs. Albee (1959) did a manpower study which showed that it was not possible to train sufficient numbers of psychologists in order to meet the need for their services. Given the number of persons admitted each year to mental hospitals, and the amount of work one psychologist can reasonably be expected to do in assessment and therapy, one can quite easily reckon how many would be needed. In this country, Likorish and Sims (1971) estimate the figure at 70,000 clinical psychologists. On the basis of a time-and-motion study done with my colleagues, I think a more realistic figure is around 200,000. Given that there are at present only about 700 practising clinical psychologists, this becomes such a ridiculous figure that there must be something seriously wrong with the therapy-and-assessment model of the clinical psychologist's role (Hawks, 1971).

Albee (1968) went on to argue for a political role for clinical psychologists, having completely lost faith in the intrapsychic models. A later American survey was to provide strong support for this lack of faith. While generally there is a shortage of mental health professionals, in some areas – notably the West and East coasts – there are heavy concentrations of them. In Boston, a survey by Ryan (1969) showed that the city was *oversupplied* with mental health professionals – it was one third above the figures recommended by the American Psychiatric Association. However, whilst 'more than 150 out of every 1,000 Bostonians are identified as handicapped by emotional disturbance, only ten out of this 150 get help in mental health settings.' Thus, the abundance of mental health specialists in no way ensured that the average citizen was getting adequate mental health care.

Thus, already by the mid-fifties the two major aspects of the clinical psychologist's skills had come under heavy attack as ineffectual. Although stimulating much debate, psychologists could see no more valid alternative roles, and so these critiques did not provoke the formulation of new methods.

The move from intrapsychic to interpersonal theories

Before the mid-fifties, almost all the personality theorists, such as Freud, Jung, Murray, Rogers and the non-directive school, and trait theorists like Cattell and Eysenck, had used an intra-psychic model from which to develop their ideas, i.e. they had studied the individual in isolation and sought the causes of his behaviour in his personality and attitudes (see D3). There had been a group called the Neo-Freudians in the '30s (Fromm, Horney, Adler) who placed more emphasis on social variables. In the '40s, Harry Stack Sullivan's (1953) theory of 'inter-personal psychiatry' had moved away from an intrapsychic model towards trying to develop one based on interpersonal dynamics. Unfortunately, his influence was limited as he was only able to write in a very complicated, almost unreadable style. However, his ideas on communication between the 'patient' and the members of his family influenced a group of mental health workers, mainly psychiatrists, working in Palo Alto, California, and in 1956, this group – Bateson, Haley, Weakland and Jackson – published their tremendously in-fluential book, *Towards a Theory of Schizophrenia*, which in-troduced a term that was to become a catch phrase: the concept of the 'double bind', which occurs when two contradictory messages are sent at the same time. Usually, one is verbal and the other non-verbal, i.e. a body cue or the tone of voice. Other conditions are that the recipient cannot or is forbidden to com-municate about the contradiction, and cannot escape the inter-action. One example they gave is:

A young man who had fairly well recovered from an acute schizophrenic episode was visited in the hospital by his mother. He was glad to see her and impulsively put his arm around her shoulders, whereupon she stiffened. He withdrew his arm and she asked 'Don't you love me any more?' He then blushed and she said 'Dear, you must not be so easily embarrassed and afraid of your feelings.' The patient was able to stay with her only for a few minutes more and following her departure assaulted an aide.

The importance of the article was that it stressed that inter-actions between people were contributory to the development of mental illness. If that was the case, then the important others in the client's life, such as his family, should be seen along with the patient, and this led to the development of 'family therapy' (Haley and Hoffman, 1957).

The interest in the family can be seen as a first step on the road to awareness of the social dynamics of mental illness. Laing's career clearly illustrates this. In 1960, he published *The Divided Self*. As 'an existential study in sanity and mad-ness', it was still essentially intrapsychic, although his insistence that the psychotic's language was understandable and not 'a word salad' was congruent with the view of Bateson *at al.* (1956). In 1964, with Esterson, he wrote up eleven case studies of the families of schizophrenics. They showed to their own satisfaction that the patient was being 'scapegoated' in order to save the parents from their own madness. (Unfortunately, they didn't use a control group, so the empirical basis of their conclusions is rather shaky.) This view was also receiving wide credence in America through the studies of Wynne, Lidz and Ackerman (see Handel, 1968), and for a few years, the concept of the 'schizogenic mother' was quite widely used. However, it was always unsatisfactory. Once you move away from intra-psychic variables, you can't stop the causal links at the mother – because what's making her the way she is? So by the mid-sixties (Laing, 1967), Laing had moved on to seeing us all as mystified and having violence done to us. Unlike the empathic clarity of *The Divided Self*, the language is now smeared with blood. We are all being driven mad. There was no way forward, so he backed off into Eastern mysticism (Sedgwick, in Boyers and Orrill, 1972).

Family therapy had as little empirical support for its utility as the intrapsychic model it was hoping to supersede but it was important in opening up the field of interpersonal communica-tion and for taking into account a much wider range of vari-ables. Psychologists therefore became more interested in seeing whether sociological analysis could be of use.

23

The development of sociological ideas relevant to the psychologist wishing to understand the context of, and the organizational restraints on, his work was a feature of the late 50s. There are two areas that were important to the development of community psychology: (1) studies of the organization of mental hospitals, and (2) the epidemiology of psychiatric services.

The first group of studies examined the assumption that the mental hospital was run for the patients' benefit and was geared to their recovery. Such writers as the Cummings (1962) and Stanton and Schwartz (1954) all examined the hospital as an organizational structure. They showed that the needs of the staff are far more crucial to what happens to patients than any explicitly stated goals of the institution. For example, Stanton and Schwartz were able to relate the ebb and flow of symptomatology among patients to the presence or absence of communication difficulties among the staff. The frontrunner of this group was Goffman's *Asylums* (1961). Here the hospital is described as 'a total institution' where the rules are mainly for the staff's benefit; the nurses, not the doctors, are in charge and essentially the patient is faced with the task of learning how to play the rules. Kesey's (1962) novel, *One flew over the Cuckoo's Nest*, brilliantly parallels these ideas in literary form.

These books all supported a view of the mental hospital as too large, too impersonal, too insensitive for the needs of the mentally ill to be met.

Turning now to the *distribution* of mental health services, Hollingshead and Redlich's (1958) *Social Class and Mental Illness* reported a study in which they took as their sample all persons in New Haven receiving psychiatric treatment at any time between May 31 and December 1, 1950. The three main findings were:

(1) The more serious mental illnesses, i.e. psychoses, were over-represented in the lower socioeconomic classes. This finding has been replicated many times in both the US and the UK (Susser, 1968).

(2) Type of treatment was unrelated to diagnosis. This hardly gave psychiatric diagnosis much of a boost since it implied that other factors were more important in determining type of treatment.

(3) The factor that strongly correlated with type of treatment was social class. The lower the socioeconomic class of the client, the cheaper the treatment he received. Thus, the working-class patient very rarely got psychotherapy, and the treatment he received (drugs, physical methods) cost far less. Since many psychiatrists are in private practice in the States and thus would have little interest in providing services to those unable to pay for them, the authors checked to see if this finding also applied to publicly supported agencies. It did.

It is an ironic fact that this very important study has never been replicated in the UK; perhaps you can guess why – even though most psychiatrists work for the NHS, the results would be the same. Even without empirical data, the clear relationship of class and type of treatment received is quite evident in this country too. The main suppliers of verbal therapy are student health centres, private practice, and teaching hospitals. The consumption of the first two is so clearly related to social class as to require no elaboration. As regards hospitals, teaching hospitals are far better financed and staffed than are ordinary hospitals, – even the patients' meals cost twice as much in the former. In addition, whereas mental hospitals only admit from their catchment area, teaching hospitals can take people from anywhere. This means that teaching hospitals like the London or the Maudsley, in working-class boroughs with the highest rates of mental illness in London (Tower Hamlets and South-wark, respectively), are allowed to give therapy to people referred to them by GPs from outside these areas. This is very convenient for the middle-class patient, who is better able to get himself referred by his GP than is the working-class patient who tends to accept what he's given. Even more important, the decision whether to give therapy rests with the psychiatrist or psychologist. Some places will only take on patients for psychotherapy if their verbal IQ is above a certain level. Since verbal IQ correlates strongly with class (Butcher, 1968), this pseudo-objectivity is a very useful discriminator. Other places don't even bother – the working-class client, especially if showing signs of psychosis, being considered 'unsuitable for treatment'.

In working-class areas, GPs are likely to be less sympathetic to signs of mental illness, and sometimes will even be unable to recognize them. They will prescribe psychotropic drugs freely to a patient they feel they can do little for to get him out of their overcrowded surgery. Thus, patients often stay on these drugs for years, an unhappy state of affairs when some of them, like barbiturates (sleeping pills), are highly addictive. The psychiatric out-patient clinics, sited in rundown general hospitals, are grossly overcrowded and thus the sessions with the psychiatrist are of a few minutes duration only. The session will mainly focus on the effects of the patient's drugs. Frequently, the patient, taken in by the publicity of the drug companies, some of whom spend more on advertising than on research, is seeking a 'miracle drug'. The interview then becomes a bargaining session while the patient's plea to be put on the same drug 'as my aunt which she said made her feel so much better' is fended off by a registrar, whose command of the local idiom is often hardly adequate.

A neat illustration of the class bias in treatment is provided by the mental hospital back-up in a north-west London borough. Residents, if they need in-patient treatment, can theoretically go to one of two hospitals. One is a small hospital with a high staff ratio and offers psychotherapy. The other is a large hospital with drugs as the staple diet. The former is used far more for the middle-class patient than is the latter. It may be worth mentioning that the relationship of social class to type of treatment is by no means restricted to mental health services. Hart (1971) surveys other areas of medicine in support of his Inverse Care Law: 'The availability of good medical care tends to vary inversely with the need for it in the population served.' (see B5).

Returning to the field of mental health, it is important to spell out the implication of these facts. I have so far illustrated how the mental health professionals, being middle class themselves, feel far more at ease and prefer to treat high verbal, neurotic middle-class patients. The working-class patient often feels uncomfortable in the therapeutic situation, may see little point to it, and may well request (and certainly will usually only receive) drugs. However, since mental health professionals know that drugs alone will not help him, there should be a strong drive by them to develop new techniques which will help the less verbal, and a discontent with a status quo which tailors the clientele to existing methods; and this is one of the strongest motives behind the development of community psychology.

This concludes our survey of the historical background of community psychology. We have seen how, in the early fifties, the major revolutions of open wards and the introduction of psychotropic drugs occurred in the mental hospitals; how the role model of the clinical psychologist as assessor and therapist came under strong and effective attack on the grounds of its inefficacy, its unrealism in terms of manpower and costs, its ignoring of familial and societal variables, and for accepting the limitations of hospital organization and mores. In the early sixties, there was a great flowering of theoretical alternatives to traditional conceptualizations of mental illness. These included most of the texts we have mentioned. In addition, in 1961 Caplan published *An Approach to Community Mental Health*, outlining his concepts of 'preventive psychiatry', which we shall discuss later, and in 1962 Szasz his rather incoherent *The Myth of Mental Illness* which said you couldn't be mentally ill, as that was a contradiction of terms – you were either organically ill or you had 'problems of living' (see F8). This period also sees the emergence of 'third force' psychology, which is humanistic psychology (the other two being psychoanalysis and behaviourism) (Rogers, 1961; Maslow, 1962, etc.) (see D3).

All these texts attracted considerable support and interest, but by themselves would not have created new ways of working. Ideas are passive. Men adopt ideas when they feel the need for them, and for a profession to put new ideas into practice, it must, firstly, develop enough self-confidence for it to become self-critical, and, secondly, have the job opportunities available to apply them. It is to these two aspects we now turn.

The impetus to change

A profession has to undergo a number of stages before it can consider a major change in its self-definition. Self-criticism would seem a third stage development. The first stage is that of the pioneers. These are men of exceptional ability – Freud, Binet, Burt, etc. – who stake out the field and demonstrate the utility of their skills. The second stage is that of consolidation. The consolidators inherit the work of men of genius and thus stand little chance of living up to the promise of the profession's founders. Paraphrasing, a science which hesitates to forget its founders is going to have a gross inferiority complex. The consolidators dig in, define certain skills as central to the profession, and set up training courses where the acquisition of these skills define the professional identity. The setting up of training courses is a crucial stage as (1) it restricts admission to a field of work, thus setting up a monopolistic position which gives greater bargaining power, and (2) the selection for these courses is used to exclude those who do not agree with the definition of the necessary skills. Thus, innovation is discouraged. Gradually more people are recruited into the profession, and a career structure is created.

After a time, the role model that the consolidators propounded begins to seem more and more inadequate to the new entrants. This is partly because the social realities the profession is coping with change; partly because the new entrants do not have to wait till they have field experience to see the limitations; they can achieve this by reading the literature; most centrally, because the new entrants have more professional self-confidence. The consolidators had to be cautious because the profession was weak, and other professions were sceptical of its pretensions; now, the profession is clearly established, so one can take chances, be professionally self-critical without other groups taking advantage of it.

Besides this gradual development of professional confidence, there was also an important accelerating input – the advent of behaviour therapy and operant conditioning (see F3 and A3). (Behaviour therapy involves the application of learning principles to achieve changes in behaviour.) These were developed in the late fifties, and mainly derive from the ideas of B. F. Skinner (Beech, 1969). These techniques have shown themselves to be effective in the desensitization of phobic and obsessional conditions (see F3), in token economies in hospital wards, and most beneficially, in the development of learning and social skills by the mentally handicapped (see F2). Despite these gains, many psychologists see these approaches pertaining to a very limited model of man (see F1, F7, F8). However, in the context of professional development, this dispute is irrelevant. For the first time since intelligence testing almost fifty years before, psychology could claim ownership of a powerful new set of techniques, and this gave the profession a confidence boost.

28

This confidence and self-criticism became visible and urgent around the early sixties in America. In Britain, it is just starting. One reason for the difference is that British clinical psychology is a smaller, less well organized profession than its American counterpart and more para-medically oriented. Also, the public facilities are not nearly as disgraceful as they are in America – the hospital Goffman studied had 7,000 beds; there is much less distortion of availability of services as there is nowhere as large a private sector. Thus, American psychologists had considerably more impetus to search for alternative ways of working.

The creation of job opportunities

Some of the approaches we have discussed previously were put into practice on a small scale. Laing and his colleagues set up houses for mentally ill persons (the Philadelphia Association; the Arbours). Humanistic ideas were put into practical form by the development of T-groups and encounter groups; but these endeavours were not on a scale that could create enough posts for 'community psychologists' to develop a separate identity. This was changed in the sixties in America by the large amount of Federal and foundation money pouring into two groups of projects.

The first was the creation of mental health centres, authorized by the 1963 Community Mental Health Centre Act. Each was to serve a population of between 75,000 and 200,000 (Connery et al., 1968). This act was a clear response to the inadequacies of the state mental hospitals and by 1967, $65,000,000 were being appropriated for it (Smith and Hobbs, 1966). The same act made far more resources available for work with the mentally handicapped. In addition, parents of the mentally handicapped organized themselves into a powerful lobby, demanding better, community-based facilities.

The second group of projects was concerned with the major social problems of the inner-city areas, such as drug addiction, poverty and especially delinquency. In April, 1965, the Federal Government was funding sixteen projects to the tune of some $28,000,000 (Marris and Rein, 1974) and this was peanuts compared to the funding that was to come with such programmes as the Community Action Program, the Poverty

Program, Project Headstart, the Model Cities Program, etc. (As the bemused American public watched this stream of projects, they could at least enjoy Laugh-In's line 'If Nixon's War on Pollution is as successful as Johnson's War on Poverty, we're going to have an awful lot of dirty poor people around.')

Why was so much money poured into experimental welfare and social service projects in the inner-city areas? Why weren't these social problems tackled, not by employing social scientists, but by the more direct methods of new housing, rent rebates, better unemployment benefits, etc.? Partly, as indicated, because there were tremendous deficiencies in the mental health services for the poor; more importantly, because such direct payments were probably politically impossible and if they'd gone via the city halls, would never have got there (Marris and Rein, 1974). Piven and Cloward (1972) see these projects as basically vote-catching and job-creating exercises by the Democrats, aimed especially at the Negro immigrant from the South. Most of the programs had vote registration drives which was handy if the newly registered voter then voted Democrat, which the Negroes usually do. Secondly, these projects used a vast number of non-professionals – in 1968, 68,500 in year-round jobs and an additional 75,000 in summer. Such workers were likely to support the government that created their jobs, and it is interesting that Nixon, on coming to power, cut back on such programmes.

By the mid-sixties then, a very large amount of money and many jobs were available to psychiatrists, psychologists, social workers in the inner cities, and the word 'community' was prefixed to their titles. Postgraduate courses in community psychology were started and were heavily oversubscribed. In 1965, a crystallizing conference was held in Boston, whose theme was 'the education of psychologists for community mental health'. The next year, the American Psychological Association created a new division – Division 27, the Division of Community Psychology. The new profession had been baptised.

2
Commonalities across community psychologists

As will be clear by now, 'community psychology' is a disjunctive concept. One community psychologist might be working intensively in children's homes, another trying to improve the political effectiveness of a Negro ghetto. Even so, I would suggest that they are likely to have some attitudes and beliefs in common. In this chapter, I want to outline these commonalities and provide some examples of these attitudes in action, although the reader should bear in mind that I am inevitably generalizing.

In my opinion, the unifying theme in community psychology is that the practitioners have a different *role definition* from that of other psychologists, who they feel exhibit a 'guild mentality', that is:

> the partitioning off of human problems into guild jurisdictions and guild territories ... Psychology cannot continue to own the body of knowledge of the science of psychology, nor can education ... the methods of teaching, nor psychiatry the methods of psychotherapy ... There is a dukedom or fiefdom quality about such hard-structured power-political arrangements ... The established agencies have built strong political power bases in the community by tying themselves to their own militant guild forces on the one side and to political patronage on the other. (Rhodes, in Adelson and Kalis, 1970:30.)

The guild members buttress their own strength, losing sight of the people they are supposed to be serving. Thus, in recent times, British clinical psychology seems to have been devoting more of its energies to the issue of the registration of psycho-therapists – a monopolistic exercise – than to assessing the validity of its work.

The most significant aspect, then, of this alternative role definition hinges upon *serving the interests of the client/consumer, rather than those of the profession or its employees*. There is a more active sense of responsibility, a political commitment – besides helping the traditional client groups, psychologists should be directly involved in the social problems besetting their society. Thus, Albee (1970), in his A.P.A. presidential address:

> We have taught our students for years that mental cases include those people who are 'dangerous to themselves or others'. But we have chosen to intervene with a very restricted range of those who are dangerous to others. Who is more dangerous to his fellow human beings than the sophisticated racist? Racist attitudes and behaviour, which can be found in a great many places throughout our social and economic institutions, including our state and federal governments, are far more *dangerous to others* than schizophrenia ... If professional psychologists were truly concerned with human welfare, we would forget 'psychiatric patients' for a century and turn our attention to the psychological causes of racism, sexism and of the profit motive as sources of danger to human centered life. (Albee's italics.)

If community psychology is in the business of change – institutional and social – what are the theoretical and practical consequences of such a stance?

At the theoretical level, community psychologists would argue that a much wider range of social sciences should be considered relevant background knowledge to the practitioner. A knowledge of individual functioning in isolation is insufficient, a hangover from oligopolistic market divisions. For there to be a relatively complete theory of man's behaviour, there can only be *one* social science, not several. Thus, they freely utilize concepts from economics, sociology, organization theory, politics, etc.

There were many reasons for such a theoretical approach. It was congruent with a looser role-definition. Many community psychologists were employed in Federal projects which had clearly stated social and political aims, such as Headstart, the Poverty Program, etc., but more generally; they needed wide-ranging theories to give them guidelines for their jobs. For example, they were interested in organizational theory because they were often marginal men in established bureaucracies or working in newly created organizations, and therefore wanted pointers for such questions as: How does a bureaucracy function, formally and informally? (Here the American business school writers, like Schein (1965), Bennis *et al.* (1970), Katz and Danet (1973), were relevant.) How does one organize effectively? (Alinsky, 1971). How is political power organized in relation to mental health planning? (Connery *et al.*, 1968; Piven and Cloward, 1972; Marris and Rein, 1974).

There are direct practical consequences of this theoretical approach. Because of their greater sociological awareness and their more political stance, community psychologists have greater sympathy for the view that the deviant's 'career' is stage-managed by social agents, such as the police (Cohen, 1971), psychiatrists (Scheff, 1966; Szasz, 1962; Laing, 1967), nurses (Goffman, 1961), and social workers (Weiner, 1973).

An even more important implication was that *it doesn't make sense to regard mental illness in isolation from its familial and social nexus*. Thus, they would regard as inadequate models that place the causes of the patient's distress within himself, be these models biochemical, genetic, intrapsychic. The use of drugs by themselves to 'help' the mentally ill is particularly strongly attacked, because it disregards so many other facets of the person's life, and reduces his humanity and dignity. The role of the individual psychotherapist was, in like fashion, rejected by community psychologists.

Mental hospitals were thus unsuitable places to treat mental illness, because of their cost, inefficiency, and isolation of the 'patient' from the social network he was unable to cope with (see F3). Regarding his difficulties as part of a complex web of community stresses and living patterns (Kelly, in Spielberger, 1970), they would argue that facilities should be readily available *near the patient's home*; should be smaller so that he forms part of a meaningful group; and should better reflect the local conditions and needs. *The community is the correct base for the psychologist's operations.*

Thus, one of the community psychologists' main goals is *effective alternative ways of helping the emotionally disturbed outside the hospital/medical framework*, and *within the com-*

munity. Fairweather *et al.* (1969) took over a motel and filled it with chronic patients, most of whom were psychotics, with on average over four years' stay in mental hospitals. At first, it was supervised by a psychologist whose task was to get autonomous group living going and set up work-crews who ran a janitorial service. Gradually, the psychologist was phased out and two laymen supervisors were brought in. Although some of the residents were on regular, and sometimes very heavy, medication, during the three and a half years that the project lasted, readmission rates were very low. Cowen *et al.* (1968) organized a programme whereby maladjusted children were given sessions with a retired person; research indicated these were beneficial. Project REED, Tennessee (Hobbs in Carter, 1968), provided disturbed children in care with teacher-counsellors, backed by psychologist consultants. The residential centres were in the community and were open twenty-four hours a day for parental visits, and children went home as frequently as possible. Poser (1966) hired college students, few of them studying psychology and none with psychotherapy experience, to take groups of schizophrenics one hour daily for five weeks; on the battery of tests given, these groups showed significantly more improvement than those taken by experienced psychiatrists, social workers, and occupational therapists.

Similarly, if the psychologist's function is to relieve unnecessary psychic distress, then clearly people should not have to crack up before they receive any assistance. Thus, another emphasis in community psychology is on *the need for preventive services*. Self-help groups of people at risk – like widows/widowers, unmarried mothers, parents of subnormal children, etc., should receive support and advice. People undergoing biosocial crises (Caplan, 1964), such as births, bereavements and operations, should be given help so that they overcome these crises and do not become mental health casualties. Store front clinics, with walk-in services are quite widely used, since they place less physical and psychological distance between the client and the mental health professional (Adelson and Kalis, 1970). Such projects often hire local persons, as indigenous workers, to make contact with client groups, e.g. drug addicts, unemployed adolescents. Thus, generally mental health services should be more widely and more readily available to members of the community.

So, a crucial aspect of community psychology is that *the psychologists will be involved in a wider range of activities, applying psychological methods to a far greater variety of clients/consumers than previously.*

One of the activities that community psychologists are far more likely to involve themselves in than other applied psychologists is *planning and policy-formation.* Some working in large bureaucracies, realized that, without this role, they had no chance of influencing the way services responded to the needs of, and were delivered to, the local population. Other community psychologists, feeling that it would be too difficult to gain this role inside the large bureaucracies, deliberately chose to work for voluntary organizations, community groups, or independently funded experimental units. From such bases, they feel they stand a better chance of applying pressure on existing services. Whichever option they chose, both groups were aware that a fieldwork role itself was insufficient to cause structural change.

Another important change in role-definition is the development by community psychologists of the *consultant* and *skills-transmitter* roles. The *consultant* role allows the psychologist to advise a large number of persons about their work and thus potentially influence the care/treatment of many clients (Caplan, 1970; Cook, 1970). Much consultation work is now done with teachers and nurses. Besides advising on children and patients, psychologists are also advising on such topics as group development, new buildings, how to minimize the effects of slum clearance, etc. (Adelson and Kalis, 1970; Canter, 1974). Again, with the consultant role, it is clear that the psychologist is rejecting the individual therapist role for himself in order to increase the impact of his skills through their transmission by other workers.

Consultation is not only with other professionals. Even more significant is the use of *consultancy with community groups.* Thus, Ryan (1969) provided support and advice to a group of mothers campaigning for their welfare rights; Kalis (in Adelson and Kalis, 1970) advised local groups in Chinatown, San Francisco; Sarason *et al.* (1966) provided psychological backup to Community Progress Incorporated of New Haven, which created new job opportunities for unemployed, uneducated residents. This last project was completely administered by local people.

The consultant is usually attached to an ongoing service. He sees its members only intermittently and his role is mainly advisory. Thus, his opportunities to teach others his skills are somewhat limited. A more radical role is that of a *skills-transmitter, who teaches others to do what he can do* – he breaks the monopoly of psychological skills by psychologists. Previously, the teaching of psychology to other professions, like nursing, was superficial. The psychologist transmitted '*knowledge*' about psychology. He very rarely transmitted *skills or methods*, so the nurse hearing about psychoanalysis or behaviour theory was in no position to apply it. Now it is common for nurses and teachers to be taught the *techniques* so that they themselves can apply them to patients (e.g. Carkhuff, 1969).

Again, the community psychologist does not only work with *other professions*; he also will focus on training *members of the local population* to undertake therapeutic or helping roles. For example, Carkhuff (1969) trained Spanish and Negro neighbourhood leaders in group-facilitation. Cowen *et al.* (in Guerney, 1969) trained students to work with disturbed children in elementary schools; and there have been many other such schemes training local volunteers to work with troubled children, e.g. the Big Brother scheme (Lichtenberg, in Guerney, 1969; Cowen *et al.*, 1968).

These examples illustrate the transmission of skills to functioning members of the community. Another form of skills-transmission mobilizes groups of people who are traditionally the *recipients* of help. Thus, delinquents, ex-convicts and ex-drug addicts have been trained for social work and teaching jobs (Pearl and Reissman, 1965; Grants; in Adelson and Kalis, 1970). These are *New Careers* projects. One of the most spectacular was the Vacaville project where eighteen men from San Quentin 'most of them serving terms for robbery and violence, and some virtually illiterate' were given intensive training in the poverty and welfare fields. They were considered to have an 85 per cent chance of re-offending within a year, but in seven years only one did. The rest went onto new careers, some doing remarkably well and rising to become the heads of agencies (Hinton, 1973) (see also pp. 95–101).

Finally, there is now far more involvement of relatives as active treatment agents. In the psychodynamic mode of working, they were a nuisance to be kept at bay and uninformed, whilst the psychotherapist got on with the real work unhindered. With the advent of operant methods for helping emotionally disturbed and handicapped children, parents have been actively encouraged to learn the principles of behaviour modification and to apply them with professional support to their children (Guerney, 1969). Thus, at the termination of treatment, parents are equipped with skills to handle new difficulties as they arise, without having to return to the psychologist.

The overlap of skills-transmission and preventive work will be apparent, especially where transmission is directed at the community. Also apparent by now is the very real change in the tasks the community psychologist undertakes compared to his more traditional colleague. Little of his time will be spent in individual therapeutic sessions. Much more will be spent on influencing policy and consultancy. Working with community groups, the psychologist's time may be spent sorting out welfare rights, working on group cohesiveness, and providing support and training to key individuals. Thus, the role of the psychologist becomes much more *diffuse*; he can no longer be recognized by his testing kit or the 'hmm's' and 'tell me more's' emitting from his interviewing room. Are community-based workers then still 'psychologists'? Libo (in Adelson and Kalis, 1970) raises this point:

> Many psychologists have shed their detached, peripheral roles regarding human and social improvement and have conducted community programs of major significance. Sometimes they are asked if there is anything distinctively psychological about what they are doing or whether they, by becoming activitists, have blurred their identities and become generic 'mental-healthers' or 'community-development specialists', indistinguishable from their counterparts in other disciplines.
>
> We need not be worried about ... this question ... He is identifiable by his function more than by his discipline presumably because *society values the doing of real jobs more than it does the identification of professional territoriality.* His academic ancestry will be appreciated when it contributes to his success in community programs. (My italics.)

3
Aspects of community psychology in Britain: I

In the last chapter, I outlined some of the characteristics of community psychology – the greater political commitment; the greater sense of accountability to the client/consumer; the greater use of the ideas of other social sciences, so that mental illness or handicap are not seen or treated at only one level of analysis; the changes in role definition: the psychologist as planner, consultant, and skills-transmitter in addition to more traditional skills; the desire to make applied psychology available and useful to a wide range of the population, not just certain narrow groups of deviants, and that such services should be near the populations they serve, and non-medically oriented.

In this section I shall give examples of ongoing work by British applied psychologists. Few of them would consider themselves 'community psychologists'. While the selection of these particular psychologists is inevitably arbitrary, I hope the examples I shall give will illustrate the scope there is for a wider role for the applied psychologist in this country, and demonstrate some of the central attributes of community psychology in action. I have tried to give the feel of working in this area by the use of interviews, which were carried out in the spring of 1975.

Skills transmission: the training of nurse therapists

It might seem surprising to describe a project that is taking place at a teaching hospital since such institutions contradict many of the criteria outlined above as characterizing community psychology. However, it is a good example of skills transmission, whereby members of a less well-paid prestigious profession – in this case, nurses – were taught to become extremely proficient in behavioural techniques. The project, funded by the DHSS, was set up by the psychiatrist, Isaac Marks, and the psychologist involved was Dick Hallam. *Dick Hallam (DH)*: I graduated from Bangor in 1965; I'd switched from forestry to Joint Honours in philosophy and psychology. I went to the Institute of Psychiatry, did a clinical diploma. Then I went to Canada for one and a half years – mostly testing, not really doing therapy. Then I came back to do a Ph.D., which I finished in 1971 and took two temporary jobs at the Bethlem, one with adolescents, one with drug addicts and I realized how frustrating it is for a psychologist to work in hospitals. Then a job came up with Isaac Marks training nurses as therapists. It seemed a good choice as nurse training was in the wind at the time. I took up post in January 1972, a few months before the start in order to prepare some teaching material ... I prepared a lot of standard forms for assessment. I thought as we were going to see a lot of patients, anything up to a hundred at a time, we needed a very quick reference system in order to know what was going on with each patient; also because there were only a couple of supervisors – myself and a psychiatrist, Joe Connolly, who stayed with us for the training phase of the project.

We were dealing with a mainly neurotic out-patient population. We wanted to confine ourselves to phobics and obsessionals to begin with as we had data from previous trials with which to compare the efficiency of our therapists. (A phobic is a person with an exaggerated fear of a variety of normal social situations, such as eating round a table, speaking in public or to strangers, etc. An obsessional is a person who exhibits compulsive behaviour in order to decrease his forebodings regarding certain unpleasant but unlikely events – MPB.) But, apart from these groups, we accepted patients of all kinds – shoplifters, stutterers, enuretics, a gambler, people with what would be called personality disorders; later on, we saw a lot of people with sexual disorders. As Isaac Marks is quite well known, he had acquired a long waiting list of about a hundred patients. A psychiatrist had to see all patients to give them an assessment interview and then pass them onto us. About 80 per cent of them were considered suitable for behaviour therapy (see F3); and of that number, 15 per cent refused treatment; and a further 15–20 per cent dropped out of treatment. Most were referred by GPs.

M. P. Bender (MPB): How did you select your nurse therapists?

DH: All were registered mental nurses with some experience, in their mid-twenties. We got about eighty inquiries, twenty firm applications, nearly all men. We selected the final five on the basis of previous initiative, maturity, and flexibility. Their average IQ was 119, which is higher than the average nurse's. None gained financially by coming into the scheme. We paid them as charge nurses or ward sisters; and all stayed for the three years of the project.

The first two weeks were an orientation period – talks, seminars and films. They also saw other therapists demonstrate treatment with in-patient obsessionals. They practised desensitization on each other. (Desensitization is the graded exposure of a person to an object/situation that he fears – MPB.) After a bit of modelling (modelling is demonstrating by example to a person on how a situation can be effectively handled – MPB), they were thrown into the deep end. We aimed to provide each therapist with a graded experience of therapy, by starting with simple cases like specific phobias and working up to more difficult cases. We used mainly *in vivo* approaches rather than imaginal approaches with phobic patients (see F3).

Treatment often started on the first day they came to see us. About 85 per cent were out-patients, 15 per cent in-patients. The in-patients, particularly obsessives, were problems where you needed extra environmental control.

MPB: So the first time they came in after the initial screening, they saw a nurse?

DH: Yes, we decided that as the nurse was going to be the therapists, they had to be seen as such by the patients, as had we been involved in any way they would immediately attach themselves to us being of higher status ... in fact, I don't think most patients even realized their therapists were nurses, although they'd been told; nobody really objected.

My job was looking after assessment measures, the evaluation of the research, the teaching of psychological theory, and the supervision of therapy with Joe Connolly. Generally I would discuss the case immediately before the session, clear up what things the nurse therapist was going to do. Occasionally, I would sit in on the session, and sometimes when there were problems I had to jump in. For example there was a spider phobic who was rather histrionic and the therapist couldn't cope. He didn't have the authority to push her into the phobic situation. All she needed was a firm hand. Perhaps he hadn't graded it properly. You have to introduce these bigger steps very subtly.

MPB: They were pretty highly motivated?

DH: I was really surprised at their motivation at times. They would get a patient with a new kind of problem they hadn't dealt with before and they would take home six reprints and read them over the weekend. I mean there's nothing like having to deal with a practical problem to motivate people.

The simple cases in which they achieved success were very important in building up their confidence; they learnt how to relate on a one-to-one basis with patients, and they gradually learnt a professional stance. Then we introduced more difficult cases – agoraphobics with marital problems, obsessive patients on an in-patient basis – obsessives are I think the most difficult neurotic patients to deal with (see F3). Nevertheless, we achieved a respectable degree of success with the ones we saw, so the therapists were reasonably encouraged. After that, the next stage was social skills training. We brought in a few outside speakers interested in the topic, we ran a few seminars, and started our own self-training group. We'd role play social situations together as a group, videotape it, play it back and we'd comment on how we'd reacted in the role-play situation, which might be returning a defective article to a shopkeeper or showing you're pleased to see someone after a long time. We were teaching people to show warmth in a personal interaction; how to be appropriately assertive.

MPB: So how many sessions before you threw them in the deep end again?

DH: About three or four seminars, three or four training sessions.

MPB: What were the problems they were given?

DH: Well, one guy was a garage hand who was quite competent and would have been promoted, but he wasn't sufficiently assertive. When people came up to complain about their repairs, he couldn't answer them back. He couldn't direct men, was incapable of giving other people orders. So it was really simply giving him information, what to say, how to say it and giving him practice in these situations. By the end, I can't remember if he was promoted but he was much happier, much more assertive. Usually, socially phobic individuals can't sit round a dinner table with people, don't like going to parties, can't talk to men or women and have very low self-esteem. The two I had most to do with came because they had problems of eating in public, and that was the reason they basically came, because they couldn't go out with their boyfriend or girlfriend to eat. We took them down to the local restaurant – after a little persuasion. The girl was anxious for half an hour, we stayed for an hour. After a while, she felt more confident in the situation. Next time we got her to order the meal and complain about the food to the waiter. They both improved moderately. They'd lost a lot of the restrictions on their social behaviour but they certainly didn't become A1. The girl got married. Then she decided she didn't want any more treatment, because she'd got married and didn't have to go out.

MPB: Were relatives brought in?

DH: Most definitely. We always brought in relatives where they were relevant and sometimes we would directly involve them in treatment. Don't forget that most of our patients were out-patients and we were very much involved in the community because we involved patients' spouses and relatives, although certainly less than half came from Camberwell.

MPB: So how many social skills cases did the nurses have?

DH: They saw about two or three each.

MPB: We're now six to nine months out?

DH: Yes. We had planned that they should treat sexual problems but the Ethical Committee of the Maudsley decided that the nurses shouldn't be doing this. They had some fantasies about nurses paying domiciliary visits and eventual scandals. Anyway, after nine months they said you can treat secondary sexual problems but not primary sexual problems, so if a person, whose primary diagnosis was agoraphobic, also had (secondary) sexual problems, that was OK but not if they were primary ... we saw quite a few sexual problems in that way and after eighteen months they said 'Yes, OK, we think you've proved yourselves, now you can deal with primary sexual problems'.

MPB: Is that the range of skills?

DH: Yes, except for cognitive techniques, such as self-management – we tried to incorporate self-management techniques into treating phobics.

MPB: How do you manage yourself?

DH: Part of it is what you say to yourself in the phobic situation. Do you say to yourself 'Christ, I'm scared. What's going to happen next? I'll never get out of here alive.', or do you say to yourself 'It's not as bad as I've known before. If I keep calm and breathe deeply, I'll feel more relaxed.' So we'd teach them these self-control techniques like breathing deeply, saying things to themselves which would be more consistent with a coping attitude than a worried attitude. We taught them to rate their own anxiety on a 0–8 scale which helped, so they could label their feelings.

Quite frequently, the therapist travelled to the patient's home area because that was the important area for them to deal with. But we never actually visited the agoraphobics in their homes. (Agoraphobics are people who have a fear of leaving (the security of) their home and whose fears, mostly of open spaces or crowds, usually increase with distance from home – MPB.) We tried to avoid this at all costs as we didn't want to encourage a dependent attitude on us – we'd meet them somewhere in the neighbourhood.

They also got some experience in marital therapy, not much. It had to be included as quite a lot of neurotics have marital problems and you can't really avoid doing something about it. We used a learning kind of model – a materialistic contract-exchanging approach. I think a mutually beneficial exchange is a prerequisite to any relationship. Often marital relationships seem to be disrupted by something as trivial as the husband refusing to build some shelves in the kitchen. It seems very trivial, but this could be the focus of their marital difficulties.

MPB: Surely it was an expression of their difficulties? It was a message about their relationship.

DH: OK, I agree there was another message but the point is: can you get them off this negative spiral blaming each other for what they don't do and get them on a positive feedback spiral and gradually building up a sense of trust.

MPB: Presumably the marriage hasn't collapsed too far.

DH: If they wanted out, we tried to work out some amicable agreement between them.

MPB: Were you behaviour therapizing your staff?

DH: I've seen quite a few reports from the States where they reinforce the staff with green shield stamps and an extra ten cents an hour for putting in more effort. That's far too mechanistic. Our staff had feedback all the time which was positive or negative depending on how they were doing ... in fact, we had too much motivation going, they were too competitive. They were too keen to prove they were good therapists and better than the next man. They were very strong personalities.

New patients were interviewed by the therapist, with the other four nurses, the psychiatrist, myself, watching through the TV monitor. This was quite threatening, but a good learning situation. So in fact, they were able to observe each other's mistakes, and refine their interview techniques.

MPB: What was the unit's attitude to drugs?

DH: In most cases, we took them off drugs unless they were on anti-depressants or really needed them. So if they were on tranquillizers, they were taken off them.

MPB: Can we turn to results?

DH: We dealt with about 200 cases. Marks referred two-thirds of all his new referrals to us. 110 were agoraphobics or specific phobics or social phobics or had social skills difficulties; about 30 were obsessives; about 20 miscellaneous; 40 sexual, mainly primary. We usually had two or three targets per patient, things that would produce a significant gain in their lives. We would pick targets of desired behaviour change which were feasible – not necessarily at the top of the hierarchy; it could be half-way or two-thirds of the way up. (A hierarchy is an ordered series of situations increasing in their power to evoke anxiety/fear – MPB.) Most agoraphobics have other phobias such as claustrophobia, hydrophobia, etc., and these could be the other targets. Of those who had an adequate term of treatment, something like 70 per cent benefited considerably. The average number of sessions per phobic was eleven. We can compare these results for phobics with half a dozen previous trials, conducted by psychologists and psychiatrists, using desensitization of various sorts; and all we can say is that the nurse therapists do as well. In fact, they come out slightly better.

MPB: What was the effect on the Maudsley of these highly successful junior staff doing well at things they shouldn't be doing well at?

DH: Initially, there was quite a lot of feeling that they were playing at being doctors and psychologists, but later on they commanded more respect. We were very isolated as a unit and this was an important element in our success, simply because we didn't have to give a damn about what the hospital thought of us. There was a little friction on the in-patient wards – a psychiatrist might suddenly change drugs or might tell the patient to go home for the weekend when this wasn't planned. The nurses sometimes resented the nurse therapists with their special status coming onto the wards.

Marks started on this project two years before it got off the ground. He was at committee meetings, was arguing the whole thing out with the Chief Nursing Officer, who was against the project to begin with. Now she's right up to the hilt in backing it. This sort of scheme needs a psychiatrist backing it, if only to get funded – there are no psychologists in the DHSS, as far as I know.

MPB: The future?

DH: The first two years were devoted to training, and the third was a secondment phase to see how feasible the nurse-therapist role was in the NHS. After two years, we found places for them. Two of them ended up in teaching hospitals, attached to consultant psychiatrists who funnelled cases to them. One was offered a job in the psychiatric wing of a general hospital and when he refused it, they offered it to a clinical psychologist. One went to a general practice for a short while before going on to be a nurse tutor and he was offered £4,000 to stay with them. I think the other four will be able to find jobs as nurse therapists. Over the last year, we've been part of a panel devising a syllabus for the Joint Board of Clinical Nursing Studies which approves all postgraduate nursing qualifications. It is now almost completed and should be out in a few months. This means that any hospital can now run a course in behavioural psychotherapy. In the early days, a psychologist will probably be the main training person. Leeds might run a course, Manchester, maybe Birmingham. We'll run a second course – the money's definite.

The main objective's been achieved. We've now set the thing up on an institutional footing. My feeling is that there are thousands and thousands of psychiatric nurses who could be much better employed than they are at the moment, doing a lot more good for the patients they see and a lot of them are crying out for training.

MPB: And yourself?

DH: I was offered a principal's job at a prestigious hospital, which included setting up a new day hospital. I can imagine myself going to committee meetings every other week, battling it out with bloody psychiatrists, bashing my head against the wall – it's just not worth it. I'd say it'll be another five to ten years before the psychiatric profession is sufficiently weakened to allow any sort of takeover. I don't think the time is ripe – the question is: who plans therapeutic services? In the meantime, clinical psychology is a depressed, oppressed field, where all the best people have left or got out.

Taking Hallam's last point, he is referring to the fact that at the end of the fifties, many of the best British clinical psychologists emigrated to much better paid jobs in the Commonwealth; also that 'if a person changes his post and leaves the NHS region in which he is working then there is at least a 50 per cent chance that he will be leaving the employment of the NHS' (Kear-Colwell, 1972), i.e. ceasing to be a practising clinical psychologist, since the NHS has a near monopoly on clinical psychology.

Two points may be made about this scheme. The first is that, in common with many such training schemes, there is a problem of how these nurse-therapists can practise these skills fulltime in a career structure which has no such posts. (In nursing, as with most professions, seniority takes you away from client contact.) Secondly, one must bear in mind that this was a pioneering project, so motivation and group cohesion are likely to be high, and the results better than when the novelty has worn off.

Overall, we can see that in about eighteen months, the nurse-therapists received a very wide training in behavioural techniques, far superior to anything that a trainee clinical psychologist could hope to receive. Not only was the transmission of skills well handled, the recording and assessment techniques were well designed to study their progress with patients. Again, organizationally, it was sound since it was isolated from outside interference. It has been a successful prototype for other courses, not just a one-off as is the fate of so many such projects. Doubtless, the prestige of Marks as the psychiatrist in charge had a lot to do with this.

(This section is based on an informal talk I gave to educational psychology students at Southampton University, March 1975.)

If 'community psychology' has any meaning to clinical psychologists in Britain, it is probably taken to mean *not* working in hospitals away from their catchment areas; so Social Services Departments are often seen as providing a better base of operations and a wider range of opportunity. At the moment, there are about twenty-one clinical psychologists working in these departments but most are in managerial roles. There is only one department in the country with a strong team of clinical psychologists doing fieldwork – in the borough of Newham, in the East End of London. It has an establishment of three 'community psychologists', soon to be four.

It might seem surprising that a poor borough like Newham should have this number of psychologists. The reason is that Dr. Dennison, who was MOH for twenty-five years after the war was very interested in mental health and developed the services. There were of course educational psychologists in child guidance, so he applied that model to the adult side, and they advertised for a psychologist in 1968. Psychologists weren't very interested in this sort of work at that time, so although I was fresh out of university, I pretty well got the job by default.

Three years later, in 1971, as a result of government legislation, based on the Seebohm report, the Social Service Department was created. It was an amalgamation of two previous departments, Children's, and Welfare which was responsible for the elderly and the physically handicapped, and meals-on-wheels, and the Mental Health Division and home helps service, which had been sections of the Health Department. This made one very large organization. In 1974–5, this department had a budget of £4 million and that's half of what some of the richer boroughs are spending. It employs about 1,600 people in three main divisions:

(1) The Casework Division contains all the social workers, who are organized into three area offices. Each area office serves only a given part of the borough. (So the first thing a client is asked is 'Your address, please', since if he 'belongs' to another area, he is directed to the office of that area.) Before the amalgamation, his differing needs were dealt with by the three different departments, so if you were having difficulties with your child,

you went to Children's, with your grannie to Welfare, and if you felt your nerves were bad you went to Mental Health. The policy *now* is that one social worker should deal with all your social needs, and social workers are trained 'generically' rather than in a single specialist field.

(2) The Residential Services Division is responsible for all the old people's and children's homes. In 1974, these contained 745 and 150 persons respectively. It is also responsible for the hostels for mentally handicapped children and adults, and a large hostel complex for the adult psychiatrically ill.

(3) The Day Care Division has numerically the largest services, namely home helps and meals-on-wheels; also the day nurseries and six training centres for various groups of disabled.

While the quality and quantity of services will differ from one local authority to another, you should find the services I've outlined in each, as they're statutory.

I'll briefly review possible advantages of working in a local authority rather than a hospital setting:

(1) *Obviously, you're nearer your client population*. This means that you are likely to see clients at a less advanced stage of their careers as 'mental patients', and certain techniques – *in vivo* behavioural techniques, family therapy – are easier to undertake. You are also more accessible to your clients, and thus potentially can intervene more quickly and more appropriately in their ongoing problems.

(2) *You are closer to other necessary resources*. Few clients have only mental health problems. Thus, you often require the services of social workers, social security officials, housing officers, etc. Because you either work for the same department or the same local authority, you are likely to have a better knowledge of available services; and it's also easier to get hold of the necessary services as you're often known personally to the relevant officials, and are not just a voice on the end of a phone, a signature at the bottom of a letter.

(3) *You can work with a very wide range of client groups*. As you will have gathered, Social Services has a very broad mandate and is legally bound to cater for a very wide range of groups. Thus, given the interest and skills, you can work with groups not usually within the traditional clinician's orbit.

(4) *You are offering a less stigmatized relationship*. Most people can't tell a psychologist from a psychiatrist and don't like psychiatrists, with their powers to compulsorily admit. In a

Fig. 1 *London Borough of Newham: Social Services Department*

		Director		
Assistant Director DAY CARE Division	Assistant Director CASEWORK Division	Assistant Director RESIDENTIAL SERVICES Division	Chief Administrative Officer CENTRAL ADMINISTRATION	APPLIED RESEARCH SECTION (N = 8)
Principal Assistant	Principal Assistant	Principal Assistant — Principal Adviser		
	Area Group Organizer Area 1 (N.W. Ham), Area Group Organizer Area 2 (S.W. Ham), Area Group Organizer Area 3 (E. Ham)			

Day Care — Major Responsibilities
*Day centres: for the elderly (N = 70), the mentally ill (N = 150), the physically handicapped (N = 150), the mentally handicapped (2; N = 70 and 120; workshop for the blind (N = 30),.
Meals on wheels
*Day nurseries (4)
Luncheon clubs; holidays
Departmental transport
Services for the physically handicapped, and the sensorily handicapped
Psychological services

(social work teams)
Casework — Major Responsibilities
*Family Casework services and assessment of need for all groups of clients
Hospital social work
Playgroups
Child minders
Work with juvenile courts

Residential — Major Responsibilities
Children's (Community) homes (N = 170)
Old people's homes (N = 745)
*Hostel complex for the psychiatrically ill (hostels (25) bedsits (8) flats (19)
*Hostels for mentally handicapped children (N = 19) and for mentally handicapped adults (with nearby housing) 2 psychiatric group homes (N = 8)
Residential nurseries
Inspection, registration of voluntary homes

Applied Research — Major Responsibilities
Applied research
Training
Community development and liaison

* Areas presently serviced by psychologists (N = 4; 2 full-time in Day Care; 2 working ⅓ of their time in each of the three divisions.)

49

Social Services Department, you are seen as part of the (old) Welfare Department, which has a much friendlier image, since seeing a social worker does not brand you as insane. Thus, people may be more willing to discuss problems with you.

(5) *You have a more independent role*. In a hospital, the clinical psychologist is essentially a para-medical. In Social Services, your boss is a social worker, not a psychiatrist. Also, there is no problem with direct referrals to psychologists as this is standard for social workers. Finally, since these departments were only created three years ago, their organization is more fluid than that of hospitals, so one has more say in defining one's role, especially as few people will have stereotypes about it, as they tend to have in hospitals.

These then are some of the advantages of working in a Social Services setting. Returning to Newham, for the three years after 1971, there were two psychologists working in the department, Anthea Johnston and myself, and it was in this time that the psychological service was built up and took shape. One thing that was clear was that the traditional ways of working in clinical psychology weren't going to get us very far. Clinical psychologists didn't seem to have really asked themselves how they should structure their work to be maximally effective. They didn't seem to focus their work on maximizing the well-being of people they reckoned they knew something about. They'd accepted the assessment and therapy role and there wasn't much evidence for either their validity or their utility. With the exception of behaviour therapy, there's not much evidence of psychotherapy being effective. So, on the therapy side, Anthea worked with a GP practice, providing behaviour therapy for phobics, and we later widened this service to accept referrals for agoraphobics or social phobics from anybody. Otherwise, we do very little individual psychotherapeutic work.

On the assessment side, I wasn't going to waste our time providing bits of type for the files. But in fact that's not where it's at. Assessments *per se* can be good or bad – that's a matter of your clinical skills. What matters is what happens *after* the assessment – that your recommendations, if sensible, get implemented. If they don't, that's when it becomes a waste of time.

What I came to realize was that, as long as we were working within the individual model, seeing clients all the time, we'd never change the quality of services. A few lucky clients would feel better but nothing else would change. We had to get to the point where we were influencing the nature of the service itself. We obviously would continue working at the client level but in addition we needed to get ourselves a policy planning role. It became clear that we had to work at various levels – the junior social workers, the care assistants in the centres and hostels; the heads of these units; and the HQ staff. I call this 'multilevel' work because you are trying to influence the bureaucracy at various levels of seniority, and the nature of your work varies according to the level you're working with. Within the centres and hostels (the first two levels), we work on 'projects'. You can't hope to have any impact if you try and service all the centres and all the hostels. There are 170 mentally handicapped adults in our centres alone. So, the only way two psychologists can be effective is to work with the staff to create a therapeutic environment in *a part of the centre/hostel*. I made it clear that while we would offer a crisis service at the individual level, most of our work would be in the form of projects. In a project, what we do is to select, with the staff, a small number of clients and work out a programme that will increase their mental health or independence, or whatever it is we're aiming at. Then we work closely and intensively with the staff to make that programme as effective as possible – a 'total push' philosophy. For example, Anthea and a senior member of staff at one of the training centres for the adult mentally handicapped set up a pre-work unit that could take a dozen or so trainees, as a token economy. (A token economy is a system whereby certain behaviours are reinforced negatively or positively by tokens which can be cashed for money or desired goods or activities.) Within a year, we got a dozen clients with IQs of less than 50 out of work permanently. In the hostel for the adult mentally handicapped, I'm working with four staff on twelve residents who we reckon can live independently. We're giving them domestic training and group discussions in the hostel; and for those who don't go out to work, but go to the training centres during the day, I'm ensuring that they get training there. When the flats around the hostel have been built, they will live in them as small, independent groups. In ten psychologist-years at Newham, we have undertaken about nineteen projects. Other projects include the management of a psychiatric group home, the preparation of clients living in the hostel for another group home, and the setting up of a linguistic and educational unit for mentally handicapped adults.

A very important point about projects is that they have a limited life, after which they're thoroughly reviewed and are often stopped because they've achieved their goals. When the flats are ready and the residents move in, that project will be completed so I can move onto something else. Also, during a project, it's the psychologist's business to make sure that he is transmitting his skills to the staff, so that he becomes more and more redundant as they become more competent and confident. Thus, his time investment should gradually decrease. So the project concept allows you to move continually into other areas of the service and develop new ideas and services.

At the senior level, we need to have a say in policy and to ensure that our projects get the resources needed. We're involved in staff selection. Obviously, we're interested in planning for new resources, and we're usually involved. I've carried out a number of fairly effective research projects into service needs and the way services are run, but generally Anthea and I got more satisfaction out of fieldwork so that perhaps we haven't had as much say as we might have. But then policy usually only makes sense when it's being applied, and we're there when that happens, so we can often modify any unpractical proposals.

To show how these various levels of working dovetail together, our work in the psychiatric day centre can be used as an illustration. We set up the reception unit where all new clients start. Here, they are assessed by a psychologist and he/she will bring their recommendations to a case review meeting, which decides on the treatment plan. Since I'm the chairman of that meeting, if their recommendations make sense, they become centre policy and must be carried out. But since I think the fieldworkers are the key people, although social workers, doctors, psychologists attend, it's the centre staff whose opinions carry most weight. At the meeting, we don't just discuss a client's mental health, but also look at problems like rent arrears, his physical well-being, the suitability of his medication, and can call in additional professional resources as needed. Besides this, we run groups in the reception unit and also set up a pre-work group. Given all this fieldwork, we are well aware of the centre's needs and if the centre needs more resources or some difficulty is bothering it, we can have a word with the principal adviser responsible for the centres. For example, if the centre gets very short-staffed, we might ask that a suitable staff worker in another centre is temporarily transferred. So, we're operating at the level of the individual client, backing up the staff and at the organizational level.

Another aspect of our work is that it is 'wide range'. As I see it, we have a given set of skills and these are available to anyone who wants to use them. So we'll accept referrals from anybody and work with any client groups we feel we can help – the mentally ill and handicapped obviously, the old, the physically handicapped, children in day nurseries, and homes, and so on. At a more exotic level, we've advised vicars and chiropodists. On the other hand, we wouldn't accept a referral where we didn't feel we had the relevant skills.

This is an important point. A psychologist should work out the likely pay-off of his intervention and see if it makes sense and whether it'll change things. You've got to work out whether a request is genuine, or your presence is to make councillors happy, whether the staff will work with you – that sort of thing. For example, at the time of the amalgamation, we thought we should look at providing services to the old people's and children's homes, but the former were so understaffed and the latter so claustrophobic, we reckoned it would take us years to have any effect, so we moved into other areas. I'd like to think that we've got across to the Department that professionalism entails the right to say 'no', but although no one ever asks us to do something we don't want to do, I think this is because we work one third of our time in each division (i.e. casework, residential, day care), and so it's very hard for them to argue we have the time for new work; and also because they probably think 'there's no point, they'd only do it badly and sulk.' It's negative power. I'd like to see psychologists move towards contract work with a hiring agency as Alinsky (1971) suggested for community workers, as I think this forces both parties to be explicit about the terms of the agreement, and accountable for their work. Perhaps this could come with area teams of clinical psychologists, but it's probably too radical and requires too much honesty.

So far I have talked about influencing services through project, multilevel, and wide range work. In addition, we have a management function. I assess applications for residential accommodation in our hostels for mentally ill and mentally handicapped people and we chair a fair number of meetings.

This management role gives one power to get things done. Then, as well as working with staff at all levels, we work *across* the three divisions. We are almost the only people to have this freedom (most people are employed to work in only one division). Thus, we have a great deal of information about what's going on and also can sort out problems that go across divisions. Information and the ability to short-circuit the cumbersome march of a problem up the hierarchy of one division and down the hierarchy of another are good sources of authority. On the negative side, though, this sort of work is unpredictable, time-consuming and not very satisfying. I think we're getting sharper with people and, rather than doing such work, we try to advise people on how to influence workers in other divisions.

Limitations of our approach

A more serious and less solvable difficulty is that we have both a management and an advisory role, and it's sometimes difficult for staff to relate to both these roles simultaneously. I don't see how we can avoid it. I suppose we could say to the staff, 'Well, of course this is only my opinion, which I'll be giving to the Assistant Director', but if your advice keeps being put into effect, they'll know what's going on. To a certain extent, one can try and get round this by a division of labour, so that I'd take the organizational, policy role and my colleagues do the field-work. However, I think they'd resent me preaching while they practise. Also, I feel very uneasy advising about things where I haven't done any fieldwork. Besides, I'm too young to die.

At the project level, one has to avoid the problem of over-extending oneself. I think we now know that our best work is done with groups of 10–15 and initially needs at least ten hours field and organizational work per week going down to around six hours after three months. So that can be planned for. What can't be planned for, and what's almost inevitable, is that project work creates structural stress within an establishment. As we're only working with one part of it and not trying to provide services across the board, the other staff feel deprived of our services (if they think we're any good). We probably know some of their clients and *could* usefully help. So we have to spend some time backing them up and this blurs the project concept, but is necessary if their resentment is not to hinder future projects.

At the HQ level, senior staff have to be at least neutral about what we're doing, and there can be an awful lot of reasons for them saying 'Very nice, but not today'. We need to be kept informed by them and to be seen as part of their team. At the unit level, it's essential to have the support of the head or otherwise we can do little, and he/she can help minimize the misunderstandings and jealousies I've been talking about. At the fieldstaff level, there has to be some slack, because the introduction of new ideas and methods upsets the routine, requires record-keeping, etc., so staff need some spare time to try them. I think it's important to realize that psychologists *create* rather than save work, because at least in Newham, they're pushing for higher standards, better services, and this requires more work and more concentration than is needed with a custodial role. So the staff must have the motivation, and also the interest in our ideas. Thus there are an awful lot of necessary conditions that have to be fulfilled before we can work optimally.

This means that in Newham the maintenance of the psychologists' morale is of great importance, perhaps more so than is usually the case with hospital psychologists who have a more predictable environment. I'm becoming more aware that if we're going to work in this way, we have got to build in strong formal and informal support systems. In addition, it's important that the team maintain directionalities. It's too easy for staff meetings to degenerate into catharsis and information-swopping sessions, and while on the surface that seems adequate, I suspect it's a killer, and an insidious one; because what happens is that one loses sight of long-term objectives and gets bogged down in day-to-day crises and can't see any movement. So, what one wants are staff meetings where one discusses things like 'what should the ideal psychiatric centre and our services to it look like?', and works out very long-term goals. But that's difficult to do if one's used to responding quickly, and to medium-term (project) planning.

The future

By the autumn, we'll be a team of four psychologists and probably two students, so one task is to form a cohesive, effective service with these large numbers. I intend that we work intensively in an old people's home and really show what can be done, so it doesn't look like an undertaker's waiting room. Another project I'd like to start would involve providing a psychological support service for the intake team on one of the social work areas. The team deals with all new referrals and tries to sort out their problems within a three month period. (After which, the case is either closed or referred to a long-term caseworker.) I think psychologists should have something to contribute there. Clearly the areas we move into will depend on the interests and skills of the people in the team, just as psychological services to the day centre for the elderly were developed by Alison Cooper as this was a field of interest to her.

The most definite thing is the opening of a purpose-built 150-place mental health centre. We'll have some say in its policy and it'll have the equivalent of one full-time psychologist, if not more. I've got two ideas I'd like to see in action, which are slightly contradictory. The first is the formation of a very strong assessment team of psychologists, social workers, and centre staff. Each new referral would be treated as if it were a crisis point in the client's life, so that a thorough and wide-ranging examination of the client's needs would be made and programmes developed to help him, both in the home and in the centre. This leads onto the creation of a number of differing therapy groups catering for different types of clients. So you might have groups for anxiety cases, for poor communicators, for role-playing work and social situations, for mothers having difficulties with their children, etc.

The other idea stems from the strong feeling I have that the days of specialist units for the mentally ill are numbered, due to the very great social stigma. So, it's essential that the place doesn't only serve the needs of the mentally ill but those of *local community groups*. It's a large building with plenty of rooms and could be available for such groups in the evening. Also, it's rather foolish to concentrate all one's attentions on the sick part of mentally ill people, because it maintains them in the sick role. So I'd like to encourage clients to form and run their own interest groups. So, with the local community coming in and the clients themselves running activities that would interest the local residents, one could get a very livening interchange and intermingling. This would focus on the clients' skills and interests, not their deficits. How this could co-exist with highly directed therapeutic efforts I'm not sure, but I'd sure like to find out.

I am concerned that we have done relatively little research on our efficacy. The department doesn't expect it and because of our work load, it tends to get skimped. Another problem is the nearly complete lack of decent assessment techniques for the mentally ill, so this means we will have to spend quite a bit of time devising our own. However, if we don't research our efforts, we are depriving ourselves of valuable feedback and the chance to assess our work in greater depth. I would like to see us build in research techniques which specify which areas of a project we are succeeding in and where we're failing. With students doing their placements with us, it should now be possible to be far more research-conscious.

Overview

I am often asked why we call ourselves 'community psychologists' and the reason is that I didn't like signing myself simply 'psychologist'. This was when I started and had no idea what 'community psychology' meant. Later, when I got to know what the term meant, I thought of trying to work more directly with the community but I realized that, bureaucratically, I wasn't in a very good position to do so, and, more important, I didn't have many skills to offer vicars, youth leaders, tenants' associations. It would have been a con, even if my bosses had let me do it.

The next question usually is: well, are you any different from other clinical psychologists? And the answer is yes and no. Yes, because I'd employ anyone who had the skills needed here, whether their background is educational, clinical, or even untrained. I've offered a psychologist post to an ex-psychiatric nurse who I thought had the potential to develop into a good psychologist. Unfortunately, she was working as a social work assistant – the sort of slave class of Social Services – and got scared by the status difference. No, because I think whatever we're doing here that's useful should be applicable to other institutions. If Newham is of interest to other psychologists, it would be because we've tried to work out a more effective model of how applied psychologists can maximize their influence on the services offered to client groups, rather than accepting the traditional, quiescent role we're trained in.

For ourselves, I think we've now clearly established the utility of psychologists to Social Services, and moved to a position where we can influence policy, especially at field level.

I know that certain things would not have happened if we hadn't been here – the psychiatric centre is more therapeutically oriented, the subnormal centres have reasonably strong social training programmes, the hostels are more open to community needs than they might otherwise have been, and so on. It doesn't seem much, but that's the way it is, because the staff you've trained up go on to better jobs and your successes fade back into the community.

2: The Child Treatment Research Unit, Birmingham

The next example is, I think, particularly valuable in outlining the difficulties psychologists have when taking well established techniques into new settings. The project, funded by the DHSS and Birmingham Social Services Department, and headed by Derek Jehu, Professor of Social Work at Leicester University, had two main aims: to test (1) the utility of behavioural techniques with children in the context of a Social Services Department, and (2) the utility of the 'triadic' model. This is a psychologist-as-consultant model, the triad consisting of the *consultant* who advises a *mediator* (who could be a professional or a relative) on how to help a *target person* (Tharp and Wetzel, 1969). In this case, the mediator was a residential or caseworker and the target person a child in some form of care.

The two clinical psychologists involved, Keith Turner and Roger Morgan, are both very experienced in behavioural techniques. Whilst these have been widely used in hospitals and out-patient clinics, they have not been applied, in this country, to the residents of children's homes on any large scale. Their first project was a control trial on enuresis (incontinence of the bladder). After systematically sampling the children's homes, they formed two groups of twenty children – one to be treated, the other to act as a control group. They used the bell and pad method (Mowrers, 1938). This trial was successful. All but one child stopped wetting. They intended to move onto a similar trial on conduct disorders (aggression, physical assault, disruptiveness, etc.) Here, however, they ran into difficulties. In what follows, I shall describe what I feel these difficulties were, although the psychologists themselves might not agree on every point.

(1) The project was inappropriately sited. Birmingham Social

Services Department is responsible for one and a half million people, has 4,000 staff, 100 children's homes and has 10,000 children in some form of care. To try and change the ways of one of the largest local authorities in the country in three years seems a trifle ambitious.

(2) Given (1), the project was understaffed. The establishment was for three psychologists. In fact, for most of its life, it had only two. Scaling up from the Newham experience, it seems likely that this project needed a team of some half dozen psychologists if it was going to have any impact.

(3) The project took place at an unfortunate time – shortly after the amalgamation of the three departments into Social Services. The problems of integrating three departments with very different ways of working were great and caused much stress among the staff. In Newham's department, in 1972, a conservative estimate of the number of social workers on minor tranquillizers and anti-depressants would have been 25 per cent. One effect, across the country, was a high staff turnover. This makes the consultancy role inappropriate for a number of reasons:

(a) If staff turnover is high, then due to the time it takes to replace staff and the inexperience of new staff, the Department is understaffed. This means that case-loads become larger. The average case-load in Newham for this time was 40–60 cases. In Birmingham, the problem was even more acute. Case-loads were often 70 to 80. Case-loads of this size mean the social workers are doing little besides crisis work. They certainly won't have the time to work out treatment plans. Therapy becomes a luxury.

(b) In an overworked department, mental health gets low priority. This is because there is little statutory work in this field, excepting compulsory admissions, while the work with the elderly and especially with children includes a great deal of statutory work. Thus, junior social workers will be told by their seniors to cut down on non-crisis work.

(c) High staff turnover means that one can never build up an ethos where the ideas and skills can be picked up from, and discussed with other social workers. One is continually starting from scratch. Skilled staff, being in high demand, are particularly likely to leave.

There is a more general problem. Operant techniques demand that the therapist has control over the patient's environment and can prevent or negatively reinforce responses he considers anti-therapeutic (see A3). For this reason, such techniques have been most useful in situations where the patient's freedom of action is restricted and his reinforcers clearly under staff control – hospitals, prisons, schools; or alternatively where the 'therapeutic agent' can create such conditions, e.g. parents with young children. In many of the cases that social workers are asked to deal with, such conditions of control do not apply and thus the social workers may not perceive the psychologists' attempts to improve their treatment skills as particularly relevant to their day-to-day work.

Let us turn now to consider the difficulties of applying behavioural methods in the children's homes:

(1) In order to set up the trial with conduct disordered children, Turner and Morgan did a screening exercise, using Rutter scales (the Children's Behaviour Questionnaire which is a screening device for children with behavioural and emotional disorders) and the Hill-Walker Behaviour Problem Checklist. These scales are filled in by staff who know the children. Scores above a certain point indicate that the children need help in given areas. When the psychologists started discussing these cases with the staff, the staff didn't feel these kids were really in need of help.

What seemed to be happening was that, in effect, the homes were organized in a hierarchy of tolerance of disturbance and violence; and a difficult child would move through the system till he reached a home where his behaviour was normative, where the staff were used to coping with that level of difficulty, and where they saw that as their job; not 'treating' the child. Moreover, reducing a child's aggressive behaviour may be counter-productive to his adjustment in a violent environment.

The disturbance-tolerance phenomenon that the psychologists found is a very important point for work in residential and day care institutions. It is all too easy to project one's own standards regarding acceptable levels of aggression, sexual activity, etc., onto the staff, and erroneously assume they will agree with you on the need for action.

(2) Another interesting phenomenon was that successfully treating a child could handicap its placement. Houseparents had very real control over who they accepted. If they found that a child had been treated, they assumed it would relapse and thus would refuse successfully treated children!

(3) In the children's homes, the familiar problem of staff short-ages again arose. The psychologists – being research workers using techniques which rely on accurate charting of baselines of, and changes in, behaviour – were keen that good records should be kept. Short staffing meant that this was very difficult to achieve. Staff similarly felt that they had not the time to undertake therapy. This was exacerbated by the fact that the psychologists tended not to be called in till a crisis had arisen and the staff were demanding the child's removal. On the oc-casions when they were prepared to consider a therapeutic intervention, they certainly weren't going to hang around gathering baseline data, so the psychologists were forced to go straight into the therapy stage. The psychologists were thus hampered by trying to apply a research design on their work.

Short-staffing and lack of motivation thus meant that the Birmingham psychologists had to abandon hopes of applying a consultancy model and do most of the therapy themselves. This involved them in wider issues such as appropriate place-ments for their child clients. Over time, the role became more one of a highly skilled case-worker. This was probably in-evitable in the circumstances, though one might suggest that the project might have been helped if someone in the higher echelons of the bureaucracy had personal responsibility and involvement in the success of the project.

Overall, the Birmingham project is extremely informative just because it was working against such odds. It demonstrates the limitations in generalization of well-trained techniques when taken out of nice protected environments like university labs or teaching hospitals. They clearly showed that there is a need for behavioural techniques in children's homes and that these can be successfully applied. (Besides the enuresis project, they also took on a fair number of individual cases, showing a wide variety of disorders.) Their success runs counter to the pre-conception that children in children's homes are so damaged that they can't be helped.

At the time the project was undertaken, my guess would be that the most useful role for applied psychologists would have been an organizational and staff support one, trying to improve staff morale and decrease turnover. However, the Birmingham experience does allow us to draw conclusions about the neces-sary conditions for the successful application of the consultancy model. Clearly, it needs an adequately staffed department with a stable staff who have the time to devote to considering treatment plans, keeping records, etc., and who can transmit their acquired skills informally and formally (through supervision of more junior staff) to other social workers. In addition, it is very clear that the consultancy model cannot be applied as soon as the psychologist moves in. No one is going to take you seriously, however qualified you are, till they've seen you and your ideas in action, worked jointly on a number of cases with you (and of course with high staff turnover this won't happen). Thus, developmentally, consultancy is a second-stage role in a stable environment. Turner and Morgan feel that, after two years or so, the model is now beginning to work with the Birmingham case-workers.

Social Services: non-traditional posts for psychologists

So far, we have described the work of people calling themselves and being seen by others as 'psychologists', so that although the content of their job is non-traditional, their status is the same as that of their more traditionally placed colleagues. One of the interesting lacunae of American community psychologists is that they haven't clearly realized that the title 'psychologist' limits the range of opportunities open to the role-occupant. The reason for this is probably that status-consciousness is one of the hardest attributes for a professional to rid himself of. So we have the paradox that community psychologists are all for training non-professionals for mental health posts but demand a Ph.D. training for themselves (Bennett, 1965). However, if we look at the posts available in Social Services, it seems clear that places like day centres, hostels, nurseries, etc., provide excellent opportunities for psychologists to try out new ideas and techniques and widen their experience; and the number of such places is continually increasing as local authorities fulfil their obligations to build them. With their strong paper qualifications, psychologists would often stand a good chance of getting senior posts in such establishments, and the spread of psychological approaches could be an important influence for better services.

Psychiatric hostels are being built for a number of reasons: (1) psychiatrists came to realize that discharging people to tension-filled homes meant that they'd be back within a few months; (2) many mentally ill people could survive in the community without needing re-hospitalization if they lived in a supportive environment; (3) very many people in mental hospitals should not be there, as they are no longer showing signs of mental illness (although they may be showing marked signs of institutionalization). However, they cannot be discharged, as their relatives will not accept them and there is no hostel provision in their local authority. They are effectively homeless.

I talked to the warden of one psychiatric hostel, Lister Bainbridge:

LB: After coming here from Australia, I worked at the Maudsley on a research project comparing psychiatric diagnosis in England and America. The place seemed to me to be a breeding ground for ambitious professionals, and the economics of the situation were appalling in terms of the cost per week per patient. A lot of the research there was mediocre at best, and the small amount of good work done hardly seemed to justify the costs of running the place.

As the year at the Maudsley progressed, I got to feel that psychologists had attached themselves in a para-medical kind of way of psychiatry and were working directly within the medical context in the mental hospital. Given that it's commonly agreed that mental illness has got not just medical components but social, educational, familial, and also sociological, anthropological, political . . .

MPB: Yes, well that seems to include most of them.

LB: . . . psychologists were giving very, very little of their time to these other aspects. I simply wanted to get to a more direct level of operation with the patient, more grass roots, where I felt a psychologist could work much more competently; and then this job with Camden's Social Services came up to run their first project in residential aftercare.

MPB: Not before time. That's been government policy since 1959.

LB: I was provided with a large, detached Victorian house, that had been converted and furnished, with our flat at the top. There were to be two staff and seven residents. All but two of the initial intake came from Friern Barnet which is the main catchment hospital. We saw about thirty patients to select the seven; age range was 20–62, three of them psychotics (both sexes). I took up post in March, 1973, and by June we were full. We took people in pairs on a fortnightly basis, so that each individual could acclimatize himself.

MPB: What are the rules of the place?

LB: I think it's important to have a minimum number of rules. We have two (unofficially compulsory) meetings a week – a domestic type meeting chaired by a resident concerned with household management, and the other aimed specifically at personal problems. Initially, I and the staff on duty attended but then I felt I was exerting too much influence, so I stayed out of the 'insight' group.

MPB: I'd have thought you'd have dropped out of the domestic group.

LB: It doesn't seem to work that way. The psychiatric patient tends to be rather more skilled in showing insight than in directing his day-to-day activities. Because I *was* the only staff member living in, I tended to be appealed to on more mundane things in the 'insight' group and this tended to take the emphasis away from more personal aspects.

MPB: What kind of therapeutic programmes are there?

LB: We spend a lot of time with a person initially in terms of working out what is a realistic and desirable future for him, look at what kinds of therapeutic procedures are necessary, and then use whatever techniques are available. This may involve behaviour modification or individual psychotherapy with somebody outside the hostel, or roleplaying, etc. I've already mentioned the groups. One of the advantages of a living-in situation is that the staff spend a lot of the time with the residents in the house doing things with them, like gardening, cleaning up, going to places, museums, etc. (This contrasts with the more usual practice of psychiatric hostels of insisting that during the day a resident either goes to work or attends a day centre – MPB.) All the house eats together. Cooking's done on a rotation basis, involving both staff and residents – the standard's been very high. So these activities build up self-esteem and a sense of responsibility about the house. We've got a fairly good staff ratio and we don't push people too hard but rather wait for them to initiate things and respond accordingly. We have a lot of art materials – lino-cutting, paints, tools, fabrics, sewing – and try to provide enough stimulus for people to get interested in things and then, hopefully, continue them outside. We also usually have six volunteers on our books at any one time and try to build up natural relationships between them and the residents. Unfortunately, they tend to go more for the non-psychotic, as they're more responsive, so some residents tend to suffer.

MPB: There seems to be a conflict between the nice, straight guy creating an easy-going group living structure and the psychologist working out individual programmes. For example, when you and your friend, who could obviously card sharp with ease, were playing poker in your flat you were joined by a friend of a resident. You two clearly didn't want him, and your friend, in a proper game, would have cleaned him out.

LB: One of the things one's faced with inevitably in residential work is that everyday, twenty-four hours a day one is exposed to being one's straight self and also having some kind of therapeutic intention and it's quite demanding in that sense. You have to learn to pace yourself but as for techniques, there are very few which have to be covert. A lot of them anyway are commonsense. If you like, each person is presented with twenty choices a day and he can either make a life-enhancing choice or an anti-therapeutic choice, and we try to load the choices. But as we're the only staff that live in, and that imposes more demands, we've bought ourselves a flat to have somewhere to escape to. Working in this area, one can readily appreciate why professionals tend to hide behind professional roles because it allows them to differentiate more clearly between their private life and their working life.

MPB: One might argue that hostel wardens create an ethos to suit their own personality. Do your staff find it more difficult?

LB: Yes. One of the idiosyncrasies of a small community is that it's very difficult to define a policy for the place extrinsically. For example, it would be very difficult for the Director of Social Services to say 'These are the rules. This is how you must run the place.' There's no kind of gestalt or group ethos, overriding the sum of the individual personalities as there may be in a large mental hospital; so the staff have quite a lot of power within their own working space and also have fewer guidelines; there's more ambiguity in their jobs and this can create a lot of anxiety. Because staff have different working temperaments, we find it absolutely necessary that we communicate honestly with each other and that we're clear in our minds what a particular programme means. Consistency's essential. We have a psychiatrist come in for one three-hour session a week. She acts in an advisory capacity, has very little direct contact with residents, except in crises. She attends the staff meeting/case conference and her role of bringing out staff grievances and differences is very important.

MPB: How many clients are working, how many discharged?

LB: None are working at the moment. We've found that a person who's capable of working is capable of living out. In eighteen months, two had to return to hospital, neither for a long stay; six have left; five are working; and one has regained custody of her child, so isn't. Generally speaking, the problem of pushing people out hasn't arisen because when they're ready in terms of having got it together, they don't want to stay and this has been something of a surprise. They feel superior to this psychiatric stuff.

MPB: Do your residents regard themselves as nuts? One of the paradoxes of hostels is that although they're not in a bin, they're still on medication, they're seeing shrinks, they're sort of halfway ...

LB: They go through phases. There are phases when they resent being seen as a patient and they find it embarrassing especially when they're building up social contact. People say 'what do you do for a living?' and I tell them to say they're artists. Also, we encourage residents to make contact with their local GPs, rather than continuing contacts with their psychiatrists, except where it's obviously necessary; and as for drugs, we believe in the minimum amount necessary. We've been reasonably successful in cutting down drug usage. About 50 per cent of those here, and of those who've left are still on them. One problem is that sometimes when a person is about to embark on a major breakdown, that's the time he insists he doesn't need medication and this was the case with the one person we really had to discharge.

MPB: What about relationships with neighbours?

LB: We've built up good links with several of them to the point where we do the usual exchanges of ladders and tools. We've had one or two acting out scenes outside the house but it hasn't damaged our relationships. They understand it's bound to happen from time to time. We've invited the vicar round several times but he hasn't turned up.

MPB: Tut, tut, a man of God. Let's go onto the future.

LB: Well, at the moment there's an awful lot of pressure on mental hospitals to decant. Since the Mental Health Act of 1959, it's been obligatory on local authorities to provide mental health aftercare but by and large this has been pretty unsuccessful. There are an awful lot of authorities which simply haven't fulfilled their obligations, and there are others which tried and have done fairly badly in the sense that they haven't fulfilled their stated aims. For example, a lot of boroughs have set up hostels which they intended to be rehabilitative, short-term but they've quickly become clogged up with chronics. We reckon an institutionalized psychotic patient needs something like four years before he's going to show any real difference and our particular project simply isn't geared to that length of time, either for clients or staff. I mean, when one's confronted with a fairly flat psychotic, who finds it difficult to contribute towards groups, leaves the cooker on, plays records over and over again in a self-mesmerizing way, indulges in incongruous laughter ... We also avoid the overt psychopathic type, who needs a lot more structure than we can provide and who'll probably always find help from somewhere. What I'd like to see is not large hostels but a series of non-purpose built ordinary houses or large flats with five or six persons. You could have a variety of residential units then. Some could be supportive for those who're not likely to get better in the medical sense. Others could be working men's hostels, others for obsessive-compulsives where there'd be plenty of scope for psychologists particularly interested in that group. The purpose would determine the staff you have. For example, it's a bit silly employing young, dynamic, therapy-oriented people to run a hostel for chronic schizophrenics, as they're not likely to enjoy their work. Another advantage is in terms of planning – you can take advantage of any property that presents itself, rather than having to wait years for a new building. Overall, I'm sure there's more self-satisfaction in this type of job than in the large mental hospitals where most of the major decisions are made by medical staff. If planning got to the stage of a number of different provisions, a psychologist, placed at a senior fieldwork level, could do readily worthwhile research into what type of hostel helped whom. I'd like psychologists involved in both fieldwork and research. This is a particularly stimulating area for psychologists because there's a lot of freedom, there are all sorts of ways of applying a clinical approach.

It was impossible for me to assess how successful the hostel was. Certainly, the residents seemed to have more autonomy and decision-making power than in larger hostels I know.

When there was a staff vacancy, each applicant was seen by at least two residents who rated them on acceptability. Agreement between staff and residents had been very high. Prospective residents spend a weekend at the house and one factor in their acceptance is the residents' agreement.

I feel that size is a crucial variable. In a larger hostel, the staff's management role is inevitably increased, (catering for thirty, for example, is a quite different exercise to catering for eight) and thus the opportunities for creating group responsibility for the hostel must decrease. Since the residents are making fewer choices and in addition are less well known to the staff, their individuality is less noticeable so that their actions are more easily construed by the staff in terms of their psychiatric condition. It's important to realize that this process may well be independent of the good-will and competence of the staff. An example of this individualization in a small hostel occurred when I was talking with LB's wife about a resident who had been very destructive and asked if they had considered having him compulsorily admitted. She replied 'You couldn't do that to someone you'd lived in the same house with for eighteen months.' (He was eventually voted out by the residents.)

There are, however, a number of difficulties regarding small, specialized units. I doubt that there are sufficient people who can run such units well, and this leads to a second problem: as the number of such units increases, it becomes more difficult to see that they are being run efficiently and honestly. (In one London borough, the warden of an adult mentally handicapped hostel was taking the residents' social security payments, and this was only discovered after a year.) Besides such straight fraud, there is an increased possibility of emotional over-involvement on the part of the staff, which can damage residents. The very real autonomy of hostel wardens increases these risks; but assuming that psychologists are all honourable men and women, it also means such posts provide considerable scope for people who want to see if their ideas work in practice. Children's homes, where the children often stay for many years, would provide such opportunities. Training centres for the mentally ill and handicapped would allow the psychologist to create and direct training and rehabilitation programmes for large numbers of clients. However, before psychologists take up such opportunities it will be necessary for them to be trained to see themselves as persons who have skills, independent of their titles. That's a hard lesson for a student, and an even harder one for their teachers.

Liverpool: educational psychology

I met the Principal Educational Psychologist for Liverpool, Colin Critchley, at a conference on 'Management for Senior Educational Psychologists' at Winchester in October 1974, organized by Jim Ward and Bob Stratford, lecturers on the educational psychology course, Southampton University. This conference was the first in the country to focus specifically on the *management* function implicit in the work of senior applied psychologists. It was interesting to see how uneasy some of the participants were at this focus, feeling that a word in the right ear, the use of informal channels was quite sufficient. Critchley, and his Assistant Principal, Ian Berry, seemed to have developed this management function successfully and also to have built up a strong service, which has many of the attributes of community psychology outlined earlier.

MPB: How does your service differ from others?
CC: Well, I think we're asking questions and we're asking the right sort of questions. There seems to be a polarization between north and south, although it's not that clearcut. More basically, it's between what I'd call Wave Two and Wave Three. Wave One were your Cyril Burts and Raymond Cattells – real pioneers. Wave Two were the people who came in after the War in the early 50s, who had a long teaching background. They saw themselves as super-teachers and now equate themselves with educational advisers. Wave Three is my generation, mid-thirties, minimal teaching experience, who see ourselves as psychologists working within a particular setting and in our case it's an educational setting. For example, in Sheffield, the educational psychologists see themselves as offering a range of skills to the whole authority, not just the education department, for example the Social Services, housing, health, by a crosscheck system of meetings. Their local authority management structure has been geared up by management consultants and the senior officers meet as a group and this is reflected in their sections, so there is a cross-fertilization; they advise on physi-

69

cal and social designs of buildings, and the needs of people. That seems the right sort of concept, although the tactics would have to be worked out locally – a group of psychologists offering a set of skills to the local authority seems to be the right type of model to develop in applied psychology.

MPB: Why the north–south split?

CC: The south had developed services and over the years these camouflaged the real needs and became rigid. In the north, because of the paucity of resources, the needs have come much more to the surface. With the local government re-organization last year, instead of six psychologists each working individually in six metropolitan boroughs, you've got the six together; and by and large Wave Three were appointed to head the outfits.

MPB: What are the right questions?

CC: (1) What unique role do I have to offer as an educational psychologist, rather than as a clinical psychologist, remedial teacher, etc.? (2) How can that role best be interpreted and implemented within the structure within which I have to work – i.e. the local authority? Having worked those out – and we still spend hours discussing them – then you can ask (3) how much of traditional educational psychology we can give away. For example, we've cornered the market in testing and built up a folklore, a myth. You could teach a bloody chimp how to administer them in half an hour.

Our plan is almost like a Russian five year agricultural plan. We set ourselves ten years. The first five years has been spent beginning training and developing the structures, the services on the ground floor. The structure's there now – a principal, assistant principal, five seniors, seven others, so you've got a hierarchy organized to take responsibility; and the service has credibility, people say 'let's see what the psychologists think.'

The second level of staff training consists, at the formal level, of them getting the full qualification – that's what I'd call quantitative training. Now we're moving into the era of qualitative training where people take special responsibility for an area and really work it up. For example, one of my staff is very interested in the toy library concept and next year, this will receive priority within our resources.

MPB: So you develop a broad range person into a sub-expert.

CC: Yes, it's like being both a GP and a consultant. You must be able to deal with anything that's thrown at you, not miss anything, but now also have a specialist role as well. So any one of the psychologists works a referral up to a certain level. Then, if it's a preschool non-communicator (usually autistics), I'd get them; SSN (Severely Subnormal) kids go to Ian, one of the girls specializes in the blind, Dave Jones in the deaf, and so on – we develop these consultative skills across the city.

Besides developing the team, another very important thing we've achieved is an integrated service working in the schools, the child guidance clinic, hospitals, and social services. In the hospitals, we work in the regional assessment centres, e.g. for SSN and non-communicating children; in Social Services, we provide induction courses for the social workers, and work in the children's homes, assessment centres and community homes (approved schools).

I specialize in preschool non-communicators – I service a hospital unit, jointly run by the L.A. (local authority) and the hospital board. I'm also interested in school phobics – desensitization and counselling of the child and his family, but now 80 per cent of my time's admin. It's not my scene at all, but it's important that the service be represented down at Central Admin. when decisions are made about new schools and new policies, and we feel we've got something to offer.

The staff do about fifty hours a week. They're prepared to work these hours because they're interested. When selecting, we chose people that have compatible views about the service, are flexible, quick on their feet and secure. Nobody's left for three years. In 1969, we spent 75 per cent of our time in the clinic; in 1973, for the same fortnight, we spent 75 per cent of our time in the community.

IB: I'd guess now that assessment covers 35 per cent of our time, treatment 30 per cent, admin. and planning 10 per cent, selling – that's running behaviour modification courses for teachers and parents of SSN kids, workshops and lecturing – 25 per cent.

MPB: You still seem to be doing a phenomenal number of assessments.

IB: We are doing too many assessments, but we're working on it. Before we'd bash away with an IQ and a reading test for each referral; now I'd like to see, as an ideal, a system that works for instance like the one in Area 5 where Tony Baldwin takes all the referrals from one school and discusses them with teachers. In many cases he doesn't take the kid out of the classroom at all. He'll advise the teachers on how to deal with them – he's particularly skilled in behaviour modification and remedial procedures for learning difficulties.

CC: Also, there are thirty-six remedial teachers all of whom have got advanced diplomas in special education. They can give almost all of the psychological tests and this is cutting down our assessment time.

IB: I see us as psychologists who contribute to education by helping individual children. We should deal with the pathologically damaged kids where psychological skills will truly count – perhaps 5 per cent of the school population. At the moment, say 70 per cent of the referrals we get are not problems that should be dealt with by us. The majority of kids we see for learning problems and truancy we shouldn't see. They'll benefit from the skills a good teacher will have – a really good and properly trained teacher, perhaps also having specific training. I mean, the truancy problem is at the top end of the school system. That'll be changed by changing the school system, not by a psychologist seeing the kid. In the long term, we see our function as having to deal with the damaged population. We may not have all the skills to do that now, but if we were able to concentrate on that population, we'd develop them.

In order to give us the time to do this, we need to advise on how to change systems, and we do it in a number of ways. The Education Department is trialling a new set of assessment forms (the Special Education forms) for the DES. We use the teacher's assessment form as a referral form. It's such a lengthy document that it cuts down on useless referrals, and also you get enough information so that the amount of assessment you have to do is lessened. Usually it's the psychologist who makes the recommendations for special education, and these go to a profile committee composed of senior admin. and professionals (such as social workers, school inspectors and psychologists). Now, the form they get – the summary form – has two very important sections: (1) recommended action, and (2) action taken. Using these, you get the authority to be aware of future educational needs. If you get twenty kids who you're recommending for a unit to train them in perceptual-motor skills, and in fact you've had to send them to ESN schools because you've got no other provision, then you can say 'Here's twenty profiles, what are you going to do about it?' In this way, we've acquired three language units, more opportunity classes (special classes in

72

ordinary schools for children with learning problems) and some adjustment classes in the city. I'm pushing for more pre-school and nursery level provision for SSN children. I've done a little exercise which shows there's not enough.

CC: In the schools, we're hammering remedial, pastoral, and guidance needs. The secondary schools must recognize that 25 per cent of the kids coming in are at risk in some area – educational, social, emotional, and they've got to build in those resources.

MPB: What role is left for the family?

CC: A tremendous one. We're not excluding them. All we're saying is that it's a fact of life that at the present time, and in the foreseeable future, a large group of kids are going to need help in some way or other, and it's no good asking the psychologist to sort out problems which are basically caused by lack of organization, structure, and facilities within these schools. These needs should be handled by a good remedial department, a good pastoral department, an adjustment unit – perhaps a school counsellor.

IB: So we've done a number of papers on reorganizing secondary schools. We're trying to get another deputy head, besides the academic and admin. deputies, who is responsible for pastoral and remedial facilities. You need a person at that level to ensure that resources go that way. Beneath him you need counsellors who are not teachers – say, one in each school – because you can't perform both functions adequately. You can't have a fellow shouting at the kid one minute, and ten minutes later 'tell me all your troubles' – it doesn't work; and you need remedial and adjustment provision in the first two years to try to overcome difficulties. You also need teacher-social workers. So you're paying attention to the needs of the children, treating children not schools.

MPB: You've mentioned behaviour modification workshops for teachers and parents. How much can you use it with children?

IB: With the SSN, 100 per cent.

CC: In school, 70 per cent of our referrals about behaviour concern the outgoing, disruptive child – the overreactive child – and the bulk of these can be helped by modification of the environment and the individual. So you have to engineer the social and support environments – and that's part of our deal – to get the right learning environment.

MPB: One of the criticisms of behaviour modification is that it makes the kids adjusted to a poor school.

CC: Well, you have to take the standards of the teacher, whatever they are – that's the reality; and when necessary, seek to modify them.

IB: But in the teacher workshops, they acquire an understanding of what they're doing.

CC: Yes, one of the things that behaviour modification does is to make them look at their own behaviour. Of course, it could be used as a more efficient form of punishment. You've got to be sensitive to the teachers and pick up signals of teachers who are going to use it purely as a control mechanism. I've never experienced this but if I did, I wouldn't go ahead with a behaviour programme; I think individual variables are the most important but I use behavioural methods because they're the most effective for the cases I get referred. Most of them are restless, distractable, so what you're doing is restructuring their learning environment and their learning set. I mean there are dangers, tremendous dangers of willy-nilly handing out these techniques. I don't know if you've seen work done elsewhere, where an educational psychologist is giving out a lot of handouts on these techniques. Now, I'm not happy with that way of doing it. I think you lose control, you're handing out techniques without adequate safeguards as to how they'll be used. But if you've got persons coming to a course for 6–8 weeks, you get a fair idea of those persons and how they're going to use those techniques.

MPB: Doesn't the turnover of teachers prevent a critical mass of skills developing in the schools?

CC: I've been doing it for four years now, and a fair percentage are still here. If perhaps 25 per cent try to spread it in the schools, that's great.

MPB: At Winchester, there was a principal psychologist who was only thirty-three. What's his career future?

CC: That's not atypical, especially among the northern group. There are principals in their late twenties, and professionally that's a problem. It is for me. In due course, I'll go back to clinical work of some nature, by a downward career move, in traditional terms – status-wise and financially. I'm very interested in working within a community and providing skills within that community for its use. One would have to be a multivariable psychologist dealing with a whole range of problems. I'm still thinking it through, how the Wave Three approach can develop further.

MPB: Otherwise, it'll go the way of Wave Two.

CC: Yes, the Wave Two people developed quite a high level of expertise in particular approaches, like the psychodynamic, and there are enough people who respond to it and utilize it to maintain the psychologists' behaviour.

Critchley is looking back over ten years as an educational psychologist for Liverpool. When he started, there was an establishment of two. What is impressive about the service is the careful definition and development of the role of the educational psychologist. They have recognized that many requests for their help are unprofitable, and have developed a clear planning and policy role in order to influence the structure of educational facilities. Also, having defined what they feel educational psychologists should be doing in the field, they have trained up a team capable of providing skilled intervention.

Also congruent with the concept of the 'psychologist as a change agent' is that they have developed services not just to their own department, but to three (Education, Social Services, Hospitals) and thus their ability to influence the well-being of their client group is greatly increased. This ability, to avoid getting stuck in one bureaucracy and to develop strong links (and eventually posts) with other relevant bureaucracies is an important and necessary feature of community psychology.

Another feature worth comment is the workshops for teachers, parents, and more recently social workers. In the teacher workshops, the teachers are trained in observation methods, gathering of baseline data, and behavioural techniques. They select a child in their classroom who is giving them difficulty on whom to put these ideas into practice. Some of the American work (e.g. Tharp and Wetzel, 1969) is quite remarkable for its bland acceptance of the teacher's definition of the situation and will work out a programme solely within that definition. It seems clear that, in Liverpool at least, the teachers' definitions of problems are critically examined and the psychologists are well aware that the problems may derive from the teaching environment as much as from the child, and will be prepared to take steps to prevent the misuse of these techniques.

Berry's work with the parents of mentally handicapped

children is probably one of the few examples of such work taking place outside the prestige teaching/research institutes such as the Hester Adrian, Manchester or the Hilda Lewis, London (see pp. 84–5). The contact was developed through the Parents-Teachers Association and the groups consist of about six parents, who meet fortnightly for about five sessions. They concentrate on social, motor and language development and emotional difficulties and are provided with assessment forms. With the psychologist, parents will work out programmes to help their child dress, eat, develop his language, etc. This is a very good example of downwards skills-transmission, and has a clear preventive role, because the parents are given skills they can apply to *future* situations. They needn't run back to the psychologist at each new difficulty or crisis.

Finally, one feature that may not have come across in the interview was the psychologists' commitment to their children. One tends to think of commitment to a cause or belief, but other dimensions of it are commitment to the locality and across time. With Critchley one almost had the feeling that the Sahara started south of the Mersey. As for time commitment, it is probably necessary to think in terms of three to five years if one is trying to create a new service, and the studied patience with which this service was built up is probably a major factor in its success.

4
Aspects of community psychology in Britain : 2

Community services for the mentally handicapped

Clinical psychologists, with behavioural and training skills, have probably more to offer in the field of mental handicap than in any other area. Professor Jack Tizard, of the Institute of Education, London, and head of the Thomas Coram Research Unit, Bloomsbury, is an international expert in this field. He is one of the most influential social scientists in the planning and development of services for this group. Thus, his work is a very good illustration of the role psychologists can play not only at the fieldwork but also at the planning level.

MPB: I wonder if we could start with what's going on in the field of preventive work in this country?

JT: There's a good deal happening in the field of mental handicap, in the way of prevention of hospitalization through good services. At the Hilda Lewis Unit, Bethlem Hospital, they're managing to keep children out of long-stay hospitals because they're providing a really adequate service on a short-stay basis; Chris Kiernan's work at the Hornsey Centre on pre-school retarded children is also relevant – if you improve the children's behaviour and their general competence, then parents are better able to cope with them; and if you give the parents support, this clearly also helps to decrease the need for hospitalization.

MPB: Can we turn to what the Thomas Coram is doing?

JT: I've mentioned Chris's work in Hornsey, which is part of it. The major part of the unit's work is a comprehensive early child programme. We think that instead of having separate centres set up by Health and Education, what is needed in any catchment area is a comprehensive health, education, and welfare centre, which would be flexible enough to combine day nursery, nursery school, and playgroup functions, and bring in a medical component as well. The research task is to see what the effects are on the families and the children. We are also looking at what problems of organization arise in such a centre, and how they're dealt with. (There are two such centres in the project – in Bloomsbury and Paddington.) In Britain, the organization of our preschool services is quite irrational. We're lagging way behind much of Western Europe, not to mention Eastern Europe, in provision. I think it's quite clear that economic needs (for more female employment) and political demands are such as to make a big expansion of them necessary.

MPB: Are the voters becoming more coherent, then, as regards the services they want?

JT: I think they are. The expansion of preschool services, which was part of both parties' manifestoes, wasn't generated by the parties but from this growing consciousness – women's lib., changes in employment and reductions in the size of families – that being a mother is no longer a career for women. The average woman who marries and has children is out of the labour force for a much shorter period of time and is much less willing than her parents or grandparents were to stay at home and look after her children. There are more mothers at work today than there were at the height of the war. Also, having fewer children leads to a very different life-style from that imposed by having children at the breast for twenty years.

MPB: It seems to me that there's no coherent approach as to what it's realistic to expect a family with a severely mentally handicapped child to cope with. On the one hand, you don't want a refrigerator philosophy – if it isn't in perfect working order, throw it out; on the other, you can't close your eyes to the stresses shown for example in your study of families with mentally handicapped children (Tizard and Grad, 1961), so we tend to offer services on a crisis basis.

JT: Well, Kushlick in Wessex is doing intensive studies on the problems parents have and he's trying to get beyond the crisis model, and he's been reasonably successful in this. They're seeing the parents pretty frequently, and, for instance, are trying to have kids put into short-stay accommodation before there's a crisis in order to short-circuit any build-up to a crisis, and also to prepare the parents so that they can part with their children and have them back again. He's also looking at the way you can assist parents in their homes with their practical problems.

Again, Janet Carr (Principal Psychologist) at the Hilda Lewis Centre has done a study of the problems families with retarded children have and this data is being used to help parents cope with them. The problem with subnormal children was well put by Farber (1960) in the States, who took some ideas from the Chicago sociologist, E. W. Burgess. Burgess saw the family as a cohort marching through life. Initially, you have your young adults and dependent children and eventually you have the Young and Wilmott (1957) situation, where the children are now independent young adults, and the parents are somewhat dependent. The problem with the severely retarded child is that as he gets older, he doesn't become more independent, so here you have a contradiction or lack of harmony between his mental and social development on the one hand, and his physical development on the other. As the parents get older, their ability to cope diminishes and so one has to anticipate a time in the lives of their children when they won't be able to live at home, and prepare them for some sort of life in a different kind of home. That's the centre of the problem.

MPB: The work you've been quoting is highly labour-intensive. It seems to me that every increment of the mentally handicapped person's performance above a certain level becomes increasingly more difficult to achieve, hence increasingly expensive, so harder to justify.

JT: I think the question is how much can you supplement publicly provided services by voluntary groups, and so how much you have to pay for all the services. But more important is the fact that, as productivity increases, you either run yourself out of work entirely, so you have the enormous unemployment you've got now in the US, or you spend a much higher proportion of your labour power on service industries, like the social services. This is in fact what's happening here, as elsewhere all over the world. For example, the size of class in school was around a hundred at the turn of this century, now we're trying to get it down to less than a third of that.

MPB: A major problem limiting the integration of the mentally handicapped into the community is that the main criterion of deviancy is work/non-work. At best, we can get perhaps 20 per cent of the mentally handicapped into employment.

JT: This has always been a very real problem – the social criterion of adulthood. When we set up sheltered workshops in the late 1940s and early 50s, we had this very much in mind. It wasn't because we thought society needed the pathetic amount these young people and adults could produce. On the contrary, we could well afford to keep them all in idleness. We sought to teach handicapped adolescents the skills that would enable them to work to show that they too could cross the bridge into adulthood. This did, I think, have an effect on public attitudes towards them. However, work may in the future become a much less relevant criterion of adulthood than it was in the past. This is happening of course and we don't quite know why. But there are more people copping out, and most people work fewer hours than in the past.

MPB: I thought the average number of hours worked had only decreased by two since the war. Could I go onto research. Where would you like to see it going in this field?

JT: You can give a whole list (Tizard, 1972), but here are two areas where psychologists can contribute. One is in demonstration projects – centres of excellence where you show what can, and perhaps should, be done; and what the implications would be for policy. Of course, demonstrations need not themselves be 'realistic'. For example, Heber's work in Wisconsin with twenty children has been very labour-intensive. He took children of black mothers with IQs of under 70 and gave them a very intensive preschool programme. Compared to a control group of children, their IQs just go up and up, so that at the age of five, their mean IQ was 120, 30 points higher than the controls'.

A second line of research involves going on from epidemiological research to looking at the social implications. Epidemiological research, (analysis of the distribution of diseases, see Arthur, 1971 – MPB), which is very good in this country, has been mostly descriptive and where it's gone beyond surveys, the main interest has been in etiology (the investigation of the causes of a phenomenon – MPB). It seems to me that we've got to switch now from studies on the prevalence of handicap to studies of the delivery, organization and effectiveness of services, and in doing so I think it's very important indeed that we should vary the services. We have never had very much planned variation in services. One of the significant things about the Wessex studies (Kushlick and Blunden, in the Clarkes, 1974) is that they *do* in fact incorporate in their model, planned variations in different forms of services. We need very many more of such studies. Furthermore, we need to develop a technology for evaluation. We've got very imperfect measures at present. For example, in the early childhood education studies in the States, the indicators of effectiveness have been, to my way of thinking, quite preposterous: whether the children can read when they're eight, or whether they passed the 11+ or its equivalent in the US, or long-term IQ changes. We've got to go beyond that and look at their attainments and the quality of their lives *at the time*; these are the important things, I think – look at short-term outcomes and process variables rather than long-term outcomes and product variables.

MPB: But what process variables are there in psychology? Our theories and certainly our measures can only handle stages, that is, we only seem to have the ability to measure psychological variables *at different given points in time* rather than *across* time.

JT: Well, for one thing I'd look at the quality of the interactions that occur, as Roy King and Norma Raynes did in their studies in *Patterns of Residential Care* (King, Raynes and Tizard, 1971). I'd look at organizational structure and child–staff interactions, and the ways in which children actually behave. I'd try to develop indicators of the quality of their play, of their language and see how this was related to the environment they lived in. This is the sort of work my wife's been doing (B. Tizard, in Connolly and Bruner, 1974), first in residential nurseries and more recently with forms of day provision for children. She found very marked differences in the children's linguistic competence depending on the type of organization that they were being educated in.

MPB: Do you think you can advance in the epidemiology of mental illness at the moment, when diagnostic reliability is so low?

JT: It's not too bad actually. There's been a WHO study on the diagnosis of schizophrenia and I think if you specify what are supposed to be the behavioural characteristics of people with schizophrenia, you get reasonable agreement. I was very struck on the Isle of Wight study (Tizard, Rutter and Whitmore, 1970), in the field of child psychiatry, that Michael Rutter and Peter Graham agreed reasonably well in their diagnostic assessments of psychiatric state.

MPB: So you move away from psychiatric classification to behavioural classification. The centres of excellence – that's always worried me because of lack of generalization; so they tend to end up as one-offs or as irrelevant status symbols. People say 'Hell, we're working with a staff ratio of 1:12, Tizard's got 1:2. We can't do what he's doing because we haven't the staff – and we can't afford more'.

JT: Here I think the pattern is first to establish that something can be done, and then try it out with ordinary service settings. The only time I know this has happened is in the Wessex region and this arose in part out of the earlier Brooklands work (Tizard, 1964) (see F2). (If examples of generalization are so rare then my doubts would seem valid – MPB.)

MPB: Can I turn to the services for *disturbed* children. What are they like?

JT: There's an absolute shortage of provision for severely disturbed children and this is a most serious deficit in our services. The preventive work is supposed to be done by child guidance and school psychological services.

MPB: Child guidance clinics seem to have got themselves into a mess because of in-fighting between the various professions and because they're selecting their cases rather than responding to need.

JT: I think that's true generally and I think one of the reasons is that they've been non-responsible or (even) irresponsible. They haven't taken on their community responsibilities (Tizard, 1973). This is what Hilda Lewis *is* doing in Camberwell. Also, in Camberwell, Bill Yule (at the Maudsley's Children's Department), Mike Rutter, and Mike Berger undertook a survey of the prevalence of disturbance among children in Camberwell, complementary to the one we did on the Isle of Wight, and they're following this up by working with schools. (Tizard, 1973, quotes figures showing that in 1965 'fewer than 1 psychologist in 14 spent half a day a week (or more) treating children in school or children's homes' – MPB.) One weakness of the child guidance movement is a lack of an epidemiological base; another is that it's been so much concerned with diagnosis. In the past, psychologists have been very largely diagnosticians or assessment wallahs and the assessment has not been very relevant to treatment. It's been more relevant to placement.

MPB: Besides psychologists not going into classrooms, another thing that seems to be missing here is involvement with the local community.

JT: I think this is very true of the whole education system. It's under much less control than in the States. The bad side in the US is that the local busybodies, the local Mary Whitehouses, can sack teachers for teaching evolution in Arkansas; but the good side is that the black women in Harlem were able to insist that the Harlem schools were changed and to participate much more in the running of the service. Here, the traditional wisdom is that the teachers teach and the parents should lay off; they shouldn't help with reading for example. In the nineteenth century, children who did learn to read were either taught by their mothers or nannies, neither of whom had a three year training, which included *some* reference to the teaching of reading. Similarly, I can't help feeling that if parents were brought into secondary schools, youngsters wouldn't be as restless as they are.

MPB: You said we should be more responsive to community needs and bring in voluntary help, but we seem to be hogging our techniques – like this nonsense about registration of psychotherapists. Also, the number of psychologists required for the kind of service you are advocating seems huge.

JT: One thing we've got to do is to recognize that a lot of the work's got to be done by parents or nurses or somebody other than psychologists. In mental handicap, people like Peter Mittler, Director of the Hester Adrian Centre, Chris Kiernan and Albert Kushlick have been very much on to this. Psychologists have a place in introducing new programmes, in advising nurses, parents, and other people – but you don't need a psychologist for most behaviour shaping. You've got to teach people to be their own behaviour modifiers if you like. Just as for example, in early developmental screening, you don't need a doctor all the time. A lot of it can be done by a health visitor, a medical student, or an ordinary parent. You're right; I think we have been very slow off the mark in bringing in less qualified or unqualified people and giving them the tools to make their own diagnosis and to get on with it.

MPB: Why do you think this is?

JT: Well, I don't think we've had much to offer in the past.

And we've never been terribly responsible. We've selected our own cases and we've never had to carry the can if a kid is suffering and we're not doing anything about it. We just put them on the waiting list.

MPB: Do you see us getting more responsible?

JT: I hope so. 'Accountability' is gradually creeping into public discussion about policy. (I was interested to find out Tizard's views on Berger's (1975) suggestion that educational and clinical child psychologists should merge into one profession of applied child psychologists. However, delicacy prevented me asking the President of the British Psychological Society such a politically controversial question.)

MPB: In terms of social conditions, i.e. certain areas are so physically grotty that they're producing psychological problems, have psychologists got much to offer?

JT: It depends on how they interpret their brief. Social policy is not really a psychological question, though it's relevant to psychology, just as it's relevant to medicine. With the help of a Social Services Department, psychologists might be able to do something: for instance, to assist in regional and area planning, to affect policy decisions on rehousing, look at alternative uses for short-life property, to ensure that that patch of ground which is used as a play-space by the kids isn't built over (see F5). This means working through Social Services Departments to influence political organizations. Policy is formed by the local council and someone's got to ensure the local council's well informed. There are two young women – Maggie Mills and Debbie Rosenblatt – who off their own bat have done a study of preschool provision in Camden. They analysed where the provision is, the adequacy of it, discussed alternatives and made concrete suggestions about where these alternatives should be placed. As a voluntary effort on the part of two psychologists, it is an important contribution, but if as a professional, you're also able to make that contribution, it should carry even more weight.

MPB: We invariably seem to work on an individual model – behaviour modification has the same faults here as psychoanalysis. We don't seem to be looking at the social structure and trying to influence it.

JT: Well, I agree with you that social and organizational problems are in a sense basic: in a Marxist sense, they're basic and the ones we're dealing with are superstructure. I'd accept that distinction and one's got to continue to point it out. However, clinical problems, individual problems are, in a different way, also basic. The clinicians work with individuals, but that shouldn't stop them looking at wider issues as well. In *Patterns of Residential Care* we didn't concentrate, as most of the American workers have done, on behaviour modification in the existing structure. Instead we looked at the organizational structure of institutions and the effects of that on the way staff behaved. I think both things are necessary – you've got to bore from both ends of the tunnel.

MPB: But we seem to do very little in the wider field. I think it's indicative that social psychology has done very little in trying to elaborate the meaning of the high correlations between intelligence and class, types of mental illness and class. Do you see any way one could go forward on that line?

JT: Well, if you're going to do that, you've got to have some kind of political understanding, or beliefs about the way in which society functions. But you've also got to have a lot of detailed knowledge about particular problems. The trouble with sociologists is that they talk in rather high flown generalizations about societies but they don't often have anything much constructive or interesting to say about how social systems work. Psychologists start with the individual and very rarely work back. We (King, Raynes and Tizard, 1971) tried to look both ways. We started with staff behaviour in various institutions and sought to explain differences in it in terms of differences in organizational structures. And we also looked at differences in staff–child interactions on the child's behaviour.

MPB: If we are to have some organizational expertise, some social knowledge, this widened training becomes longer and longer ...

JT: Well, you can read it up. I don't know about training. Nobody ever trained me in anything and I don't suppose you were taught much as a student that was of use to you when you became a psychologist ... once you get stuck into a problem, it ought to be self-reinforcing.

The very well funded are different from you and I. The 'centres of excellence' concept still makes me uneasy. Hilda Lewis House, a hospital unit for severely retarded children, is an example of such a centre. Extremely well staffed with doctors, psychologists, occupational therapists, teachers, nurses, it is impressive in the very intensive help it gives the severely handicapped child. All the numerous staff are well versed in the behavioural techniques used and work together to implement the programmes. It also provides out-patient services so that parents can be trained to handle and teach their children in their homes. They claim that 'over the past five years ... no children have been admitted to long-term hospital care'. However, this must be seen in the light of extremely overcrowded mental subnormality hospitals, which thus have no vacancies. In fact, as far as I know, there has been no published research to show the efficacy of the work of the Hilda Lewis. Such research would be extremely difficult, though by no means impossible. More seriously, the problem with 'centres of excellence' is that they are so expensive that their necessary funding could lead to distortion of service delivery. For example, as a teaching hospital unit, the Hilda Lewis accepts children outside Camberwell, and one really doubts the cost-effectiveness of staff travelling to distant parts of the home counties to see single families. One is still left wondering, then, whether spreading that expertise over areas where services to the handicapped are literally non-existent wouldn't be more beneficial.

As regards community residential provision for the handicapped, one must realize that the cost is astronomical. Newham's 19-bed hostel for handicapped children, which opened this year, cost £220,000; and unlike accommodation for the adult mentally ill, the use of non-purpose built units is much less feasible because of the special facilities required. Progress is thus bound to be slow and it is important that we do not falsely raise parents' hopes, as I think is being done by some of the more zealous organizations for the mentally handicapped. Some of the most difficult and unpleasant interviews I have had were with parents of doubly handicapped offspring who had been airily promised a place in the hostel for adult handicapped and who had to be told that, because of the heavy demand, this was not possible. (In fact, we offered them ninety days a year, the days to be chosen by them, and this has worked very well.) Secondly, however good the staff are, they are being paid for a job and have a number of children to manage and thus if the parents are reasonably caring, the child will get more attention in the home than they can get in any hostel. To my mind, then, the problem of what to expect from, and what to provide for, a family with a handicapped child remains a crucially important but unresolved issue. Jones (1974) has stressed the preventive utility of psychologists providing backup to self-help groups of parents with mentally handicapped children. One such group she works with in Camden is 'Kith and Kids' whose members with their handicapped and non-handicapped children meet regularly for social and play activities. One of their projects was to recruit forty-six volunteers to work with twenty-three of their children for a fortnight, developing their social skills. Jones and other professionals provided training and backup (Jones, 1974). She has also pointed out how frequently parents are not adequately informed about the nature of their child's difficulties, and emphasizes the importance of providing detailed and practical feedback to the parents after an assessment. Apparently, assessment centres where the assessment of the child by a team of specialists lasts a matter of weeks are being built throughout the country and will provide thorough explanations and advice to the parents (Jones, 1975).

Considering psychologists' potential contribution to planning, it worth noting that every Social Services Department is supposed to have a research and planning team, and most do. Clearly, this would be an excellent place for a psychologist who wished to develop this role. An example is Roger Morgan – remember, we met him in Birmingham? Well, he's moved – and is now head of the research division of Kent's Social Services Department.

Note again the importance of being able to move across bureaucracies. In Liverpool, we saw the psychologists providing services to three different departments. At the Thomas Coram, we see the psychologist, as an influencer of policy, bringing together three services under one roof. Similarly, in order to demonstrate the utility of such an approach, Tizard got the necessary research facilities. Kiernan's work with the parents of handicapped children, which uses very sophisticated assessment and training techniques (Kiernan, in Clarke and Clarke, 1974) should enable the parents to help their children much more actively in their development. Skills-transmission when the child is very young should yield large long-term dividends.

Preventive psychiatry

Gerald Caplan's (1964) theory of preventive psychiatry is important to the field of community mental health because it is almost the only major attempt to provide a framework of ideas that would make mental health services more effective and more oriented towards prevention. He adopted the notion of three types of prevention, which was already in use in the field of public health. One implication of this transfer of a public health model was hopefully to destigmatize and demystify psychiatry by rendering its aims and payoffs more open to public scrutiny. *Primary prevention* attempts to obviate the development of a disease in susceptible populations, so no one gets disease X; in mental health terms, to reduce the incidence of new cases of mental disorder and disability in a population to a minimum. *Secondary prevention* is based on early diagnosis of illness and prompt treatment in order to minimize its duration. *Tertiary prevention* is the limiting of an irreversible disability. Thus, working with chronic schizophrenics so that they can function in supervised accommodation might be an example (see *Table 1*).

Tertiary prevention would involve better institutional services and the novelty of Caplan's approach was his focus on primary and secondary approaches. He wanted mental health services to be fast and crisis-oriented. The idea of moving fast is contrary to the prevailing speed of bureaucracies. For example, the waiting list for child guidance clinics in Britain in 1965 was six months (Tizard, 1973; no more recent data are available). Caplan's view could be summarized as 'if you can't get there within thirty-six hours, don't bother'; because it is at the time of a family or individual crisis that intensive support and therapeutic work can be most effective in creating lasting change. If you miss the crisis time, the family will make its own, often shaky, adjustment to the new situation, which they will be very resistant to changing when you roll up six months later.

A further very important idea of Caplan's was that in the course of our lives we go through *biosocial crises* – periods of our lives when we are faced with the need for major reconstructions of our assumptive world. Such crises would be leaving school, marriage, childbirth, rehousing, prolonged unemployment, severe sickness, retirement, loss of a limb, spouse, etc. It is at such times that we are particularly liable to make a

Table 1 Types of prevention: aims, targets, goals, focus of operations (adapted from Nagler and Cooper, in Cook, 1970).

Type	Aim	Target	Goal	Focus of operations (ideal)	
				Intramural means	Extramural means
Tertiary	Limit chronicity or recurrence of illness among former patients	Behaviour change	Optimal therapeutic conditions	Client, not staff orientation	Getting funds; educating public to accept ex-patients
Secondary	Early identification of incipient mental disorder and fast therapeutic help	Community caretakers (schools, clinics, labour exchanges) etc.	Enhanced functioning of caretaker institutions	Flexible and trusting relationships within and between the various establishments	Close links with pick-up points (schools, GPs, youth clubs), easy access by community to resources
Primary	Reduce incidence of mental illness	Social system	Institutional change and community growth	Maximal role-flexibility, experimental orientation, lack of 'professional guild' orientation	Continuous dialogue between members of a community; and between community and local government institutions

poor adjustment to the now different world and this poor adjustment will make it even more difficult for us to cope effectively with other stresses and crises. To prevent this loss of functioning and the risk of mental illness, Caplan argues that preventive mental health services should be readily available to help with these cases, and since it is often possible to ascertain such persons, they could and should be actively sought out and offered such help. Thus, one programme in Boston contacted spouses shortly after a bereavement and offered them support from mature widows.

Caplan (1970) also stressed the importance of the role of consultant for the psychiatrist. If fast crisis-work was to be done, there wouldn't be enough psychiatrists to do it, so they should act as consultant to the field-staff – the nurses, social workers, etc. While undoubtedly a sound idea, Caplan does not write very persuasively on this topic, as he seems to allow very little role-diffusion – the psychiatrist still is the key figure, it's just he's a bit further from the front.

Some time ago, I had attended a Caplan seminar and one of the discussion leaders was a psychiatrist by the name of Colin Murray Parkes. I had never heard a person talk about deaths and disasters at such length and with such expertise before. (Among other things, he had provided psychiatric advice to the Aberfan community at the time of the disaster.) As he is one of the leaders in the field of preventive psychiatry, it made sense to revisit the Tavistock Clinic, where he works, to get an update on how preventive psychiatry was faring.

We started by discussing *primary prevention*. Parkes began by mentioning two government reports. The first was the Platt Report, 1959, on children in hospital, which had a major influence on the reorganization of services for children in hospital. For example, visiting hours were made more flexible, and beds provided so that parents could stay with their children whilst they were in hospital. The other report was the Finer Report, 1974, on one-parent families. Both reflected the influence of Bowlby's (1953) report for the World Health Organization on the effects of separating children from their parents, and also the films of James and Joyce Robertson, illustrating these effects. I pointed out that later research had suggested that some of Bowlby's conclusions about the deleterious effects of maternal separation had been exaggerated (Rutter, 1972), and as regards the Finer Report, wasn't twenty years rather a long time to wait to influence people? Parkes disagreed. Though important changes had taken place in some areas of work, it is necessary to wait for the older generation to die. People over forty didn't change their minds in any major way, so one had to wait for their successors. Generally, he felt that the child care services were now much more attuned to prevention and the Department of Health clearly saw this as an area of priority.

He turned then to the area of bereavement; this is a biosocial crisis for the surviving relatives and research had shown that one can isolate a high-risk group of survivors of bereavement who, if not helped, will develop psychiatric symptoms (Parkes, 1975). In Britain, a number of hospices and similar units for the care of the terminally ill were now being built. There had hardly been any eight years ago and now there were well over a dozen. He was working with Dr. Cicely Saunders and her colleagues at St. Christopher's. There the family was the unit of care, not just the dying individual. The family is encouraged to have a role in the hospice and the aim is to make it 'a therapeutic community where people can die' and where they and their relatives can work through their attitudes to death and come to terms with it. To do this, it was essential to have close staff–staff, staff–patients, staff–family links. Although there are 400 deaths there a year, and the median stay is only eleven days, in one study, 78 per cent of the relatives had felt it was like a family. This compared to 11 per cent in another, more typical hospital, without this kind of approach. He worked with a team of nurses, social workers, chaplains, volunteers offering help to high-risk relatives. These were defined by certain criteria such as having young children at home, exhibiting bitterness and anger or guilt and self-reproach, low socioeconomic status, isolation from their families, and most important was the nurses' rating of whether the relative was at risk. Seven to ten days after the bereavement, the survivors often find themselves alone, the funeral over and the relatives who came to pay their respects departed. At this time, their grief is at its height, and a visitor who will listen sympathetically is almost always welcome. Usually, two or three visits over a period of time are sufficient to allow the person to express their grief effectively and move towards reconstructing a new life. Contact is maintained by phone calls and letters. They know they can call on the team again if they want to. There is also a club in the hospice, to which they can go.

The evidence indicated that this approach could have a significant effect in preventing psychiatric disturbance. Therapeutic services were provided for half the people at high risk. At first, there seemed to be little difference between the groups but with time, as the team got better at its counselling, significant differences emerged. After twenty months of operating the service, their research showed that persons who had been counselled showed less depression, less psychosomatic anxiety and used less drugs (alcohol, nicotine, tranquillizers). There was no difference between the groups in terms of use of GPs and hospitals, but this was a contaminated measure, as the helpers had no intention of not suggesting these services where they thought they were advisable.

We discussed why such services were now necessary. In Victorian times, there was a clear cut role for the bereaved which allowed them to express their grief openly, and the family was expected to take responsibility and provide support. Also, the clergy saw supporting the widows of the parish as an important part of their job. Nowadays, they see this as less central to their work and are often embarrassed by it. Parkes did a lot of lecturing to the clergy for that reason.

Other preventive work going on included Ryle's work at the student health centre, University of Sussex. He was providing a consultation service for the tutors so that they could help their students more effectively with their emotional difficulties; some child guidance clinics are providing walk-in advisory sessions for mothers, who thus do not need to be referred by other professionals; the Samaritans' suicide prevention service has been shown to decrease the number of suicides in the towns where it operates. The organization Cruse (Torrie, 1970) creates mutual support groups of younger widows, with professional backup. These are not intended to be inward-looking; when the member has constructed a new role for herself, there is no expectation that she will stay with the group. The Society of Compassionate Friends is a self-help group run by parents who have lost a child. (There are many other such groups, e.g. Gingerbread for single parent families.) There is concern in the medical profession that GPs should reduce the prescription of barbiturates, as there are other, far less toxic sleeping pills available, such as Mogadon.

In the field of *secondary prevention* – that is, helping people with problems as quickly and as effectively as possible – there are a number of young people's consultation services, which are walk-in services (e.g. the Tavistock and in Brent). No medical referral is necessary, although the kind of client coming in is much the same as that seen by traditional clinics. The client comes more quickly after feeling distressed because there's no waiting list and because he feels less stigma. There are coffee-bars and youth clubs which have unattached social workers in areas of high deprivation, such as Hoxton, and the social workers can call on psychiatrists as required. In Boston, US, there was a barman project. Barmen are like GPs: they can either prescribe drugs or try to help, by introducing customers to each other, providing advice, referring people to the right sources of help, etc. A psychiatrist had been working with barmen to encourage more of this sort of work. At Napsbury Mental Hospital, Dr. Scott has been working on giving patients on his acute admission ward far more freedom and responsibility than was traditionally the case. Also, instead of accepting referrals from GPs requesting admission, he has developed a team of social workers and nurses, and he and members of the team visit the referred person's home with the GP. They will, if possible, provide intensive support and drug therapy to the person in his home, and this approach has cut the number of admissions by two-thirds. GPs are now welcoming the service and asking for it before the need for admission becomes urgent. The same approach is also being used by one or two hospitals with adolescent units.

Leaving the field of preventive efforts going on in the UK, I asked Parkes why, although the ideas of preventive psychiatry are fairly widely known, especially among social workers, more practice and research is not going on. He answered that for preventive psychiatry to become an effective force, it would have to become respectable and established. Although this is beginning to happen, professional attitudes change slowly and the research funding needed to establish it empirically hasn't been available. The School of Family Psychiatry and Community Mental Health, in which he was a senior research worker, had, like much of the Tavistock, been floating on American money for years. Since the Johnson and Nixon administrations, this source of funding had become less abundant. He hadn't known who would be funding his research for more than a year at a time, and it was unfair to ask research workers to work with him on such a financially insecure basis. However, research and charity organizations are beginning to think that work on the psychological care of the sick and the dying is worth funding. The Royal College of Psychiatry had started a Social Psychiatry Committee, which he thought might have some impact, so that psychiatrists moved towards doing more consultation, more planning and organizational work. He hoped that psychiatrists, as well as being concerned with people who are obviously mentally ill, would increasingly help people who are subclinically depressed and not thriving.

For himself, he intended to continue his research on illness at a time of psychosocial transition (Parkes, 1971) but also to work with the families of the physically ill, cooperating with surgeons, nurses, etc., and in the community with the primary care givers such as health visitors, social workers, community nurses.

In his own work, Parkes has tended to focus on the more unhappy biosocial crises. It is important to realize that winning the pools, getting married, starting work, all involving presumably more cheerful changes in one's major roles, are also biosocial crises. In fact, the payoff from studying these crises may be even greater than studying the more unhappy ones as they are not linked so directly with physical disability or psychological distress. Thus, their effects can more easily be studied in isolation from these other factors.

A major merit of focusing on biosocial crises is that it specifies the area of intervention and the target population, instead of attempting to intervene more fuzzily in the 'social determinants of mental illness'. Thus, it becomes possible to assess empirically the utility of one's interventions, and to compare alternative methods of helping an at risk group.

As regards the consultancy model, Caplan (1970) focuses on the psychiatrist as consultant. It would of course be grossly presumptuous of me to comment on my medical colleagues, but I cannot help wondering, since the psychiatrist's time and expertise is now so consumed by drug matters, what skills they will be transmitting?

Caplan's ideas concerning preventive work have been more influential in the US than the UK. This may be because the psychiatric profession is more powerful over there and its activities extend over a wider range. However, in this country, the Directors of Social Services Departments are, with few exceptions, social workers and therefore perhaps less influenced by his ideas. A more important reason is that the Departments are becoming the agents required to discharge more and more government policy. Thus, in recent years, new legislation concerning children and young persons, and the physically handicapped has been passed, placing heavy demands on the staffs of the Departments. Thus, their ability to set up the high-powered and flexible teams required by Caplan's approach has been reduced. However, since Caplan has shown that his ideas have utility in American welfare organizations, it would certainly seem worthwhile for the DHSS to fund the setting up of trial projects and their evaluation.

It may be useful to describe briefly the 'alternative' groups involved in primary and secondary prevention. There are houses for the patients of Laing and his colleagues (the Philadelphia Association) and for those of Berke and his (the Arbours). (There were personality differences so they split.) Both provide training in their ideas and techniques. The Arbours also has a crisis centre in Willesden, where, when a person is referred, the whole family is invited to stay for up to four weeks or so. The centre is staffed by two psychotherapists. After this, the 'patient' is referred to other sources within the Arbours, such as one of their therapists, or their houses. Fees are usually quite high. The Mental Patients' Union, which you can only join as a full member if you've been one, have a telephone advice service and three houses. They also provide legal and tactical advice about the rights of patients. A similar service is provided by COPE (15, Acklam St, W.10), who are also very opposed to psychiatric methods but being more 'hippie', seem to deal with a younger group than MPU. They run a house where they aim to support people while they 'freak'. They can stay for a month. They also publish a magazine *Heavy Daze*, which is fairly restricted to psychedelic metaphors of mental illness and later Laing. Still, it contains a fair amount of information about developments in alternative mental health groups. There are also a number of centres for encounter, gestalt, transactional analysis, etc., which will help you get back in touch with your body, for a small charge.

New careers: the Bristol project

In the US the New Careers movement was launched in 1965 with the publication of *New Careers for the Poor* by Pearl and Reissman (Hinton, 1973). The same year, the US government provided funds to implement the New Careers strategy. New Careerists are people, with poor or no educational qualifications, who have been trained for and found employment in education and social work fields. By 1970, there were 300,000 New Careerists. Frequently, they have backgrounds of prison sentences, mental hospitalization or drug abuse. There are at least four reasons for training New Careerists:

(1) Because there is less social distance between them and the community, they are better able to relate to its residents than are professionals. (This is particularly relevant when the social workers are white and the community black, since in some American cities, it is not safe for white social workers to go into the slums.) Thus, they can help those who are out of reach of traditional services.

(2) The New Careerists benefit both professionally and personally. They are able to enter professions they would normally be barred from due to lack of educational qualifications; also their helping people in difficulty often creates beneficial changes in themselves, such as increased self-confidence, less feeling of frustration.

(3) They save the agency money. Being less 'skilled', they're paid less.

(4) They save the state money. At the least, they save it paying unemployment benefits; but if the New Careerists are ex-convicts or ex-mental patients, they save it the cost of maintaining them in prisons and hospitals.

Besides these reasons, the New Careers movement has wider aims: to show that the slum-dwellers, if given the opportunities, are capable of skilled work in the welfare fields; and that their very backgrounds are an advantage in such work because of their greater understanding of the feelings and frustrations of the local community.

We have already mentioned the Vacaville project (p. 36) which helped San Quentin inmates to become New Careerists. Another such project is Community Progress Incorporated, New Haven, which hired local people to make contact with teenagers having difficulty finding or holding employment. If the latter were willing, they joined work crews. These were headed by local adults and every morning went out to various assignments. In the afternoon, the teenagers had remedial education. After this experience, many either returned to school to continue their education, to government training programmes, or to long-term employment (Sarason *et al.*, 1966). The scheme, then, besides helping local youth, provided many new career opportunities in the welfare field to local adults.

In 1973 in the UK, the National Association for the Care and Rehabilitation of Offenders (NACRO) started a pilot scheme, funded by the Home Office, to see if men between the ages of 17–21 who otherwise would go to borstal can become useful social workers. The scheme is running in a Bristol suburb, and in April, 1975, its head was Martin Seddon, a probation officer. The place, two interconnected houses, can take up to ten 'students' as the New Careerists are called. There are six staff – the head, the deputy, three linkers, and a secretary. The (rather unfortunately named) linkers are ex-offenders in their mid-twenties who act as supervisors and support to the students. Students are committed to the project, rather than borstal, by a judge for twelve months. Their training consists of a large number of placements – at least three mornings a week – in mental and subnormality hospitals, schools, youth clubs, settlements, community centres, dossers' centres, etc. In the afternoons, they have supervisory and educational sessions with their linkers. In the early days, they had a video system which the students took with them on their placements and filmed themselves when they came up against a difficulty. This was then analysed back home with their linker. Unfortunately, the video collapsed beyond repair. After six months, they gradually spend more time in full-time employment in social work schemes and new students come in, who can then be helped by the 'older' ones.

In addition, there is a 'living group' once a week, described to me by one of the students as 'a sort of encounter group', where difficulties in running the place are discussed and group decisions reached. For example, if a student wanted to go home for the weekend, it had to be approved by the group. However, how far 'the boys will manage their own lives. They will run the hostel themselves', as the NACRO blurb states is open to doubt. While there was a lot of give-and-take between linkers and students, I had no doubt who was in charge, if only because the linkers were a pretty powerfully built bunch. Besides, there had been a great deal of thieving in the earlier days, for instance of tape recorders and some camping equipment, etc. By now, there wasn't much left to take. The staff phone was locked, and the petty cash kept in the local bank's night safe, when the secretary went off.

As far as I could gather from Seddon, the project seemed to have run through three phases in its short life. The original administrator had selected delinquents with average motivation, and of the initial ten, four had gone into social work and nursing jobs and one had successfully run a hostel. Three had re-offended and two were doing jobs unconnected with social work. The administrator had then had a disagreement with NACRO and left, and the deputy took over. He wished to work with creative psychopaths, but the feeling wasn't mutual and five of the six selected were now inside. Seddon had taken over in December, 1974, by which time there was only one student. He decided to select teenagers who had the latent ability to analyse their own and other people's emotional difficulties, who had relatively stable backgrounds and whose criminal activities represented not so much a way of life but a reaction to the frustration of blocked opportunities – in his words, 'safe bets'. The system of recruitment was for the staff to go round the remand homes, talk about the project to the boys awaiting court appearances, choose from those who were interested, and then advise the judge of their willingness to take these boys. Unfortunately, it was these boys of 'good character' who the judges were most angry with and most eager to punish, so often they ignored the offer and sentenced the boys to borstal. Thus, I listened with vague puzzlement to talk of 'a good bet lost at Swansea Crown Court last week'. As a result, there were only three students at the time of my visit. However, the staff seemed fairly confident that this situation would change, since they were now sampling more remand homes and were hopeful that they would be allowed to recruit boys on bail, which up to now they had not been allowed to do.

Not having any experience in this field, I found it was hard to judge what was going on, especially as there was a great deal of borstal/prison slang I was unfamiliar with, e.g. 'a bender' meant 'a suspended sentence'. There seemed to be a good deal of controlled violence – a great deal of swearing, joke-fighting, etc. I got the impression that it was only after the students' masculinity had been established by squaring up for a fight that they were amenable to looking at alternative ways of handling criticism and modifying their views. However, I was informed that there had been only one incidence of violence since the project started, and this would be no more than one would expect from any hostel running for that length of time.

Since most of the students were articulate and motivated, and were receiving a wide range of intensively supervised placements – a far wider range of experiences at the grass roots than that of social work or psychology students – I had little doubt that they would be suitable for social work assistant jobs, if the opportunities were available. However, it seemed likely that their first jobs would be with NACRO or a similar organization, and only after that, would they go for local authority jobs.

The linkers I found a more interesting group. They were selected because their first offence was in their late teens and because they showed dissatisfaction with their former way of life. Their role seemed much more ambiguous than the students. They were supposed both to be able to relate to the students, having had similar criminal experiences, but also to the staff, with a certain role-distance and expertise to help the student. However, they hadn't had any training in social work or in teaching methods. They had no reference group of similar professionals, as they also were guinea-pigs of a new project. When they discussed their work at conferences, they found social workers, etc., unwilling to voice any criticisms, although they felt sure they had some. None of them came from Bristol, so they had to create new friendships there. Unlike the students who were allowed home only at weekends, they had greater access to their friends, some of whom thought they had swopped sides. One had been asked by a friend 'working for the police now?' and such experiences must have been common. I would guess that crimes in the house, such as ripping off the petty cash which had been a frequent occurrence, created powerful internal conflicts in the linkers, especially, as must often have been the case, they had a shrewd suspicion who the thief was. (These difficulties are almost inherent in a New Careers Project (cf. Reissman, in Guerney, 1969).)

If this was indeed the case, then the head's role in holding the linkers together is absolutely crucial. There were staff meetings twice a week, and weekly conferences with a psychiatrist who advised on group dynamics.

The linkers tended to leave when the group of students they had been supervising left, roughly after twelve months. (If a student got a local job, he could stay on a bit till he found alternative accommodation.) Of the four linkers that had changed jobs, one was now deputy of the project, one a probation ancillary, one a community worker, and one unemployed.

Seddon has recently visited the States and confirmed that the New Careers approach is by now well established. There is a career structure for New Careerists in social work agencies, and equivalences have now been worked out, so that after so many years as a New Careerist, they're paid the equivalent of a graduate student, after further experience, they're paid the same as a trained worker, etc. The job opportunities are much greater, as community work as a preventive method is taken far more seriously over there. Thus, in Massachusetts, the borstals have been closed and with some of the money saved a number of specialist social workers, with caseloads of two to twenty, had been employed, while the rest was spent on prevention programmes in the community using ex-offenders as (New Careerist) staff (Ohlin *et al.*, 1974). There was a great deal of funding of voluntary agencies, who, less afflicted by patronage and role definitions than the statutory bodies, were more free to experiment. In California, the Probation Service was paid so much for every person they kept out of prison. Thus, there was a real incentive to experiment with New Careerists, who, if successful, paid for the expansion of their numbers. Seddon thought it very unlikely that this direct transfer of funds from institutional to community services would ever happen in this country. He hoped, some time, to return to the US to study with a professor of community development, who had himself been a New Careerist.

NACRO is running another New Careers project, using ex-convicts as community workers in Hammersmith. My guess is that if the New Careers movement takes off at all, it will do so slowly due to the present economic conditions and the lack of felt political need to redeploy the poor. In terms of the prison population, it must be remembered that the New Careerists do not represent the most 'troublesome' offender, who is the less intelligent, personality disordered, persistent offender. In a sense, one wonders if the New Careers concept, in the field of delinquency, will become the 11+ of the borstals. It is hardly encouraging that the Probation Service has, as yet, not hired any New Careerists.

At the moment, the New Careers projects seem limited to the more radical voluntary agencies. As a concept, it offers tremendous opportunities for psychologists who want to start helping communities to help themselves.

Community work 1: Beckton

So far we have considered the work of psychologists and other professionals involved in teaching, fieldwork, and planning and concerned with the well-being of relatively specific client groups. However, a major theme of American community psychology is that psychologists should have a wider role than this and should become involved in welfare and social/political change. In this country, this is an approach almost untouched by psychologists. In Belfast, Ron Weiner set up the Northern Ireland Research Institute, one of whose aims was to increase the level of political awareness of the Belfast working-class community. Unfortunately, the work had to stop due to the deteriorating political situation. As far as I know, Weiner has not written up his experiences (but see Weiner in Hawks, 1976). It is the community (social) workers who have developed the activist role. They define their goals as 'improving the quality of life or the betterment of social conditions', 'giving the deprived more say in their lives'. A formal definition of community work is 'a method of intervention whereby individuals, groups, and organizations engage in planned action to influence social problems. It is concerned with the enrichment, development and/or change of social institutions.' (Brager and Specht, 1973.) Thus, they tend to work more at the large group level than do psychologists. In addition, it is often claimed that while the latter work with an 'expertise' model – they know better than the client what he needs – the community worker works within a 'participatory' model, where the client's choices are all important, and it is the community worker's job to render them effective. This argument is specious as any professional works towards goals which *he* defines (if he's any good).

It is thus relevant to our examination of the themes of community psychology to look at the skills and outlooks of community workers. As mentioned, very few are psychologists. However, ever loyal to my profession, I have selected people who either have a psychology degree or are competent mental health workers.

The first, Mike Lucas, since August 1974 has been the community worker for the Beckton area of East Ham, a physically isolated area of considerable deprivation.

ML: I did a Sociology degree and then came to work for Newham (Social Services) as a social worker. The sociology course made me think on community lines and I certainly felt that gross deprivation ought to be looked at within that perspective and not within an individual pathology/expertise framework; but the whole organization of professional services makes that very difficult. Administratively, it's much simpler to have caseloads with one person responsible. As a case-worker, I couldn't put into practice the thoughts I had about community work. Whilst on my training course, I spent some time at the Blackfriars settlement. When I came back, this job was going.

Beckton's is the Housing Department's second class accommodation, used for homeless families. The turnover's fairly high, as those who can, get out. This leaves the less able (from the Housing Department's point of view) so the place becomes more and more concentrated with young kids and unsupported mothers. It's an area which has a very few, small, expensive shops, no launderette, no facilities for the huge number of kids, poverty, etc. About 600 households.

MPB: So what did you do?

ML: The original bit of paper I produced specified four goals: (1) more efficient provision of existing services, (2) provision of new services, (3) encouraging the residents to exercise their rights as claimants, (4) the involvement of tenants in the provision and management of services.

As regards more efficient provision of existing services, when I came, a Health Visitor (HV) and an Education Welfare Officer (EWO) were already there. Now, the EWO has a statutory right to visit every household with a child *over* five, while the HV has an obligation to visit every household with a child *under* five, so between them they ought to know most single families with children. I'd already given up my statutory duties but the other two hadn't, so it was a matter of trying to help them get to grips with the community work perspective, and use what they were already doing but within a different framework. Both were sympathetic to the idea that people down there have a chronic environmental problem over and above those they have at a personal level. It was quite easy to see that there were groups of claimants who were being quite unsympathetically treated by the local Social Security office for instance, and that there were inadequate educational resources. The two local schools are thought to be two of the most 'hard-pressed' in the borough. Both workers had recognized that traditional services just weren't meeting the needs. They were spending all their time with a minority of hardcore, multiproblem families.

What I was suggesting was that we work as a team, sharing the workload according to our differing expertise. What happens traditionally is that it's pretty arbitrary whether a person goes to health/education/social services to say that their electricity's been cut off or tell them about a disturbed child or marital situation; and the service they get is equally arbitrary depending on whom they go to. If we shared the workload, we should be able to provide a far more comprehensive and better service; so the next stage was to get them to think in terms of working towards (1) getting premises in the area, and (2) working in a very task-centred way; so instead of offering personal relationships, we'd be offering a really good advice service to deal with one-off problems very quickly. Any long-term cases we'd refer to Social Services.

MPB: So you blur in the field, and any long-term case you channel back to one Department. Any hassles with the Department, with three of you referring to it, when only one of you worked for it?

ML: No, because the senior teamleader for the area was personally sympathetic, and secondly, before we referred, we'd have met the pressing material needs (leaving the social worker free to get on with the case-work).

MPB: So you would have an advocacy role?

ML: Yes, and as regards encouraging residents to exercise their rights, very much trying to get away from the practice of people coming in and saying 'we've got a problem with Social Security' and the social worker phoning them up and having a nice, friendly chat. I started taking claimants down to the local office, trying to do some modelling on behavioural lines. I refused to discuss any claimant with the SS unless they were actually present; and helped them organize appeals, where I would represent them at the tribunals. Hopefully, they will get to a stage where they can represent themselves. We also help claimants to write letters which *they* sign, on plain notepaper, so that their requests would not be treated as a matter of personal favour to the social worker. Traditionally, when the social worker makes that phone call on behalf of a claimant, I believe the claimant is left with a mystified feeling that somehow the social worker and the SS have done a private deal. They still don't really know how they've got the money so they don't know what to do the next time except go back to the social worker – it's not a learning situation. All the letters we sent out were successful and one of them was the largest payment for clothes the local office has ever made – £60.

As regards new services, we've now got premises in the area – a flat – and we've opened an office to the public. We hope to provide four or five half-day general advice sessions, and a health clinic, so you don't have to cross the A13 (a six-lane highway a mile away). In the Health Clinic, there's a lot of cheap, if not actually free, food for children. Because of all the contact we've had with all these families in the last six months, we're quite well known and popular. Once they start coming to the flat, we can get groups of people together; so that if at the Health Clinic, the HV gets a load of mums turn up one afternoon to get their babies weighed, while they're waiting, someone like myself will be in the reception room and there's an opportunity to put out ideas like a local Gingerbread group, or a claimants' group organized by themselves. Getting group pressures up within the community. There is obviously already a network of support they form themselves, but it's fairly tenuous as there's a lot of people with their own personal difficulties, which means these networks break down fairly frequently. By a neutral meeting place and some resources – at the lowest level, pots of coffee – and some sort of structure, we hope we can strengthen them and put them to definite use. At the moment, we're aiming at a group for young mothers, which will focus on welfare rights and mutual support, and run by them; a similar group for the elderly; and with local mums, and some have already agreed, we hope we can provide a crèche for the very young, so that they can go off and do some shopping by themselves.

As regards involving tenants in the running of services, there's supposed to be this split between the respectable and the non-respectable, the former being residents who've lived there practically all their lives from the time when the area was considered the best part of East Ham, and the latter the new people who've come in through the Housing Department's policy. The story goes that the two groups are totally antagonistic and there's nothing that can be done to get them together. I teamed up with Newham Rights, a legal advice centre, and we made a tape and slide show – we made a lot of colour slides, grabbed people in the streets for interviews, and edited them into a half-hour film. We then leafleted the whole area and a hundred adults turned up, and hundreds of kids to a showing at the local school. People came from every part of the area, including the stigmatized areas. At the film show, Newham Rights called for street representatives and a tenants' association (TA) committee was formed the same night.

MPB: Was this the first TA ever formed in Beckton?

ML: People had tried but not succeeded because of this respectable/non-respectable split. I think we succeeded because we used visual aids to project common problems. People could see *there was a common, shared problem – neglect.* Newham Rights is working with the TA and I've deliberately kept out because I think they've got a freer hand if a local authority representative isn't at every meeting.

We've been educating their representatives in welfare rights, and how to deal with council departments. We have a play bus – that's another new service we got for the area – which is used for the kids during the day. The Local Authority has agreed to a TA management committee for the bus, so they can use it for any activity they want evenings and weekends. The TA's organized two or three parties for the elderly. They've tried to start a campaign on housing repairs which is probably the biggest and most obvious single issue in the area. They're trying to participate in the Dockland Redevelopment Scheme. It hasn't altogether got across the respectable/non-respectable split, though. Some of those hitherto considered non-respectable are in but there's an awful lot of people among that group where self-esteem is so low that it's going to take years before they can be reached and given the confidence to join tentatively in these other things. This will be the most difficult goal to achieve.

MPB: You've provided a fair amount of material goods. What worries me about the community approach is that it doesn't reach these withdrawn, depressed persons, who one might argue rather need skilled therapeutic help.

ML: We're getting these people referred by the HV and EWO,

so we're in contact with them. We're able to provide them with some knowledge, which helps them improve their financial situation and we would hope in time to involve at least some of them in community activities. It's very difficult to assess if they need psychotherapy, when they're living in such a deprived area. A mother who may be referred to us for leaving her kids alone overnight or being a potential battering mother – would she still need skilled therapeutic help if she'd been introduced to a network of support of other mothers, had her income increased and had a structure which allows her kids to be well cared for so that she can have some time for herself? That's the point at which you can ask the question – provide that and see.

Also, I use the social work distinction of remedial work, preventive work, and enhancement. Remedial work – with somebody who's already been stigmatized so that they can get back to the position they were once at; preventive – to stop them getting into that situation in the first place; enhancement – for somebody who's not in a stigmatized position but whose quality of life is such that it could certainly be improved. It's similar to Caplan's (1964) types of prevention. You need a division of labour. Our team works at prevention and enhancement, and the remedial work is done at the Area Office. I think if you try to include remedial work, which inevitably involves statutory obligations and a social control aspect, with the other two, the conflict becomes too great.

MPB: What sort of training do you think is needed for community work?

ML: I think you want no entrance qualifications, and the Goldsmiths' course is the nearest to this. Their students also decide on course content. I mean Chas Hainey, the Newham Rights worker was a shop steward, another worker I know was a bricklayer – one wants people with a variety of training and experience coming in.

At the moment, most local authorities don't know what they want their community worker to do. Just as every committee's got to have a statutory woman, so every department's got to have a community worker. The most easily identifiable skills needed are knowledge and information. You certainly need the sort of legal and medical skill of recognizing that you can't know everything but knowing how to find it out, where to look it up. A second skill is certainly a personality one of being able to work at a lot slower pace than one is used to in any other field; being able to work with groups and not pushing them along too fast; and perhaps, having the sort of charisma that makes one attractive to the client group.

MPB: Almost all you've been saying contradicts the idea of the community worker being neutral and participatory. You've got a very clear idea of what's good for Beckton and you're working towards it.

ML: Well, you wouldn't work with a group of mothers towards a playgroup if they wanted to exclude black kids, and many TAs have said they wanted blacks out, and the community workers have had to refuse to work with them. But there's still a large element in the community worker's role of stimulating and helping to create resources that weren't there in the first place, and that's a kind of client self-determination.

MPB: What have the difficulties, frustrations been?

ML: This post's supernumerary, so in the long run there could be a problem financially. In the department, I've churned out all sorts of documents for the case-workers to look at and I've had absolutely no feedback. I know basic grade social workers have somehow to get to grips with the whole of social work legislation and practice, departmental formula and informal organization, etc. so they haven't the time to tackle the theoretical level of how the department could be organized; but it makes anyone trying to think along theoretical lines very vulnerable at the personal level, so one tends to get one's support from other community workers and from the team itself – the HV and the EWO, and at the management level from very senior social workers.

Another hassle has been the other departments. The bus has meant working a lot with the Engineers' Department who think Social Services are a load of crackpots anyway, and what the bloody hell are they doing with a double-decker bus? (Especially one they'd already converted once into a mobile training unit for the adult mentally handicapped – MPB.) How do you persuade Education Welfare that the only job they're doing is truant chasing, which they're doing ineffectively, and that they could be doing other things? The local schools think I'm a skiver for not removing kids into care. Housing measure our success in terms of rent arrears. So every Department has a different expectation. Also, because my status is so low, I can't go direct to the key people in other departments.

MPB: The future?

ML: We're now a *team* of workers down there. We've got the advice centre and are working towards a situation where the residents can provide their own facilities: their own groups to supplement the bus – their own crèche and babysitting rota, a food cooperative, etc. To build up social networks that can readily accept a newcomer and still run smoothly is a very long-term thing. I don't think we'll be in that position for at least a year and that's probably very optimistic. I think we could provide a cliquey support service before then but it wouldn't be able to take in newcomers.

The real criterion of whether we've achieved our aims is at the point at which the personalities so far involved can withdraw and those goals still be met. It's still too early to say.

In terms of community development, the last point is of course crucial. Brian Biggs, a social worker born in East Ham was pessimistic: 'I don't think he'll achieve any long-term aims. It'll peter out. It'll keep on till he goes in two or three years time and he may leave a few sparks but if they burst into flame, the Council will quickly rehouse them.' Even without assuming such political clarity on Housing's part, Lucas's work would seem hindered by the rapid and selective turnover of the population, which must surely limit the development of strong groups.

Regarding mental health work, note the practical separation of preventive and rehabilitative work. Lucas also mentioned that he felt this was not the most pressing problem for the area. More people request social service help in connection with their children and old age, than with mental health problems (this is true for all Social Services Departments). Also, there is a different weighting of priorities. Mental health workers, not surprisingly, usually see mental health as a problem having a very high priority and centrality. Community workers often see it as a secondary problem.

In terms of moving across bureaucracies, combining the resources of the three workers allows influence to be directed on behalf of the client over a wide spectrum of bureaucracy. Also since each Department listens most sympathetically to its own workers, one can utilize the appropriate worker to negotiate with a given department, independent of which member of the team is actually doing most of the work with the client. What

Tizard is doing in Bloomsbury, Lucas is doing in Beckton.

The Beckton scheme has been running less than a year, so it is too early to judge its efficacy. The memo for its wall hasn't been typed yet. Our next example is of a very experienced community team. The speaker is Bill McAlister.

Community work 2: The Islington Bus Company

MPB: Could I have a run through what you do?

BM: We call ourselves a Bus Company (BC) because we have a converted double-decker bus which is a very visible thing, and everyone knows the bus and the people who work on it; they go on outings with us, have teaparties on it, tenant associations use it for meetings, councillors their surgeries, and everyone in Islington knows they can borrow the bus. So it identifies us. We could call ourselves something like the Islington Community Development Resource Project but that really wouldn't be helpful.

We've been going for four years and are funded by Islington Council. The BC is seven people and they're selected because they have a skill we feel as a team we need to possess – one's a trained nurse who's responsible for our work with the under-fives. We've had a planner, Graham's very experienced in using video in the community. (Video is a powerful and in-expensive method of arousing local interest in issues and areas of concern to residents – MPB.) Bridget is trained in group session work, especially with young people. Our philosophy boils down to the belief that there is an awful lot that people can do for themselves and should be allowed to do. But to be able to, they need access to the same kind of support services, resources, etc., that all the big agencies – councils, government – have. It's just no good saying 'Oh, local people can do things for themselves, just let them get on with it.' Because they can't. They don't have access to the equipment, an organized office set-up, and they need that. We can cite case after case of local groups that have flourished because they've been able to call on us. We have no other basic ambitions.

So, our concern is to provide support, advice, and resources to other organizations. We don't work for individuals, only groups. There are now 400 local, voluntary organizations in Islington. Generalizing, there are two reasons why local groups get together: (1) they share a common grievance – a child's been killed on the road in front of the flats so they become more aware of the traffic problem; or their flats are in a shitty state and the council's not responding. We can provide information, help them find a meeting place, give them equipment to print notices, advise about where to send press releases; (2) they share an interest/concern to provide social and recreational facilities for people in the area. And they do this because they're concerned about the lack of them and it's something they enjoy doing. It's a lot of fun organizing a barbecue or an outing for old people. You don't need a lot of experience and it doesn't divide people. We're very keen to use recreation as a means of bringing people together, so we try to provide the necessary resources.

The resources we are able to provide are: (1) The bus: during termtime, it's for the under-fives playgroups and for childminders. It provides a stimulus and is a starting-point for setting up new playgroups and bringing together childminders. In the evenings/weekends, it's available for organizations. For example, on Friday evenings, *Grapevine* which provides a counselling service for adolescents in sex education have been using it. They'll take it to various places, put on a display, a film upstairs – a mobile advice centre. Saturdays, it's reserved for OAPs' outings.

(2) Here at the base (office), we have all kinds of printing facilities – stencils, duplicators, Xerox machine, etc. Any group can use it free of charge, except for the cost of the materials, and a policy we have which goes right across our work is that anybody who comes in and uses the equipment must be prepared to learn how to do it themselves: so we teach them and afterwards expect them to operate the machinery themselves. We also have a lot of good card indexes and information systems about what's going on in the borough. That man in there using the golfball typewriter is from a Barnsbury community action group and is preparing their newsletter. There's a whole lot of equipment organizations can borrow – a 16 mm projector, a tea urn, video, etc.

We have regular workshops in craft and youth projects once a month for all the playleaders and youth workers in the borough. The response is very good. Next month, we'll get this West Indian guy who makes fantastic masks and he'll show us how to make them with kids. Also, we do one-off training:

we had a weekend on printing and silkscreening, and recently a series on using video in community work.

Each year in the summer, we initiate projects which we'll offer out to groups. We select projects because they're exciting and interesting and we feel that the kids and adults will learn something, be introduced to something new. We choose projects that involve a skill that's not too complicated, that they could learn to do themselves. Last year, we did silkscreening of T-shirts and we offered it to all the playgrounds. We did a couple of thousand, the boys made football shirts, the girls printed popstars on them. Now there are dozens of groups that come and borrow the silkscreen equipment and do it themselves. We did the same with kites. We developed our own kite which could be made for 3p, from dustbin bags, bamboo sticks and sellotape, and we made about 3,000 of them last summer with groups, and now they come in and borrow the template. This summer, we'll do puppetry. We take on extra persons for the summer. We budget for it and we get paid to take students on placements.

MPB: What's the BC achieving?

BM: Well, I think it's achieving various things. It's something of an example of how people can work together. Our structure is relatively unique. The key is we're non-hierarchical, we're a small team of seven. There's a magic about that number. Two less, two more and you're into trouble. Five people and if one or two people go, it's a great wrench and you lose cohesion and continuity; if you're more than nine, you've got to have some kind of hierarchy. We all select new people. No one has more say than anyone else. There's no director. I've no illusions it'd definitely work elsewhere, but it works here. There has been a cost. We've been offered more money to do things which we've refused to keep down our size and scale.

Although we're available to any group – except political parties and commercial concerns – we can positively discriminate. Many local groups are using us, but of course the groups who use us most are the largest, the best organized; and when we get out our pamphlet advertising our summer projects, they reply by return of post. So we make sure that certain of the weaker groups know about it. We might take it by hand, etc. And then in areas where there are no groups to meet local needs, we have a responsibility to help initiate new ones. An old man once came in to book out the bus for a trip to Hampton Court and when I asked 'For how many?' he said 'For myself' and I said 'We're not a coach company but if you can find twenty-five old people come back.' He came back the following week. He'd gone round his flats and got twenty-five old people and that group is now meeting, has a secretary and is doing a lot of things. That's a dramatic example, but not an uncommon one.

MPB: I get the feeling that in the early days you were more active in actually forming groups – more involved in community development.

BM: No, but possibly you get that impression because since then there's been a dramatic increase in the number of groups in the borough. Partly because it's fashionable and partly because now the Council allocates money for them. So perhaps we did initiate the formation of more new groups then. But I think anybody can do that. All you need to do is leaflet an area and you can get 200 people to come to a meeting and form a group. What you can't do is ensure that the group develops and flourishes. For every ten groups that are formed by community workers, I should think nine die within a year, and the surviving one is dependent on the worker. One reason is that while a group of mothers feel confident about kicking out the chairman if he's a local, they wouldn't feel the same way about a community worker; and the community worker is certainly going to resist being kicked out in case he loses his job, or at least his credibility with his seniors.

MPB: And I suppose the BC avoid this by advising rather than leading groups. How did you get in the game?

BM: I sort of fell into it. Before going up to Oxford, I went to Algiers with a group of school magazine editors, and that opened my eyes to a lot of things, so I decided against Oxford and stayed in Paris. I wandered around the continent, did a lot of things – made a lot of money chartering out a yacht; taught English in Italy; meat portered in Copenhagen. Eventually, I ended up doing some research for a psychologist called Mednick and decided to do a degree in psychology. Since it takes seven years in Denmark, I came back to University College, London. After it, I was dithering whether to do postgraduate work. It was a seductive kind of thing because it was what the peer group wanted to do, the status thing, what the brightest did – but it bored me; but I was interested in physiological psychology and I got a scholarship to do it in Prague. That summer, I was in

America and three days before I was due to leave New York, Czechoslovakia was invaded. It was 1968. Two nights later, in a bar in New York, I met a millionaire who offered me the opportunity of setting up a travel company for young people. (I'd been a courier each summer at UC.) I did it for a year. I enjoyed it but making money wasn't rewarding. I knew I couldn't carry on without any incentive. I decided to try and sell my experience to an agency like Oxfam. I proposed that they set up a department to give advice and support to under-developed countries on tourism in a way that would benefit them rather than the Hiltons. So I came back here but Oxfam just laughed at me and said 'Old boy, that's not what we do.' A year later, partly because I had the time, I got involved in Islington, where we were living, and joined up with Ed Berman whom I'd known for some time, as the kind of No. 2 man in *Interaction*, which was half into community action and half into ego-trip things in the West End like the Almost Free theatre and expensive dramatic idiocies like the Fun Art Bus, which I think are a waste of time. (After a bitter struggle, the BC broke away from *Interaction* – MPB.) So it doesn't really make much sense. Everything was an accident.

MPB: You sound well able to float on accidents.

BM: Perhaps because I'm an entrepreneur at heart, and also when I'm in a situation I don't enjoy, I'll search hard to get out of it.

MPB: Have psychologists anything to offer in this area?

BM: I think everyone should be involved in it but I don't know what psychology can offer. It's ten years now since I was a psychology student, but I remember being incredibly dis-illusioned by what I understood social psychology to be about. I can't think of an instance where what I thought I was doing as a community worker had anything to do with psychology, or where I've ever applied anything I learnt.

MPB: Do you see your work as preventive?

BM: We're not a social welfare agency. We don't provide remedies or therapy. We run sessions with mentally handi-capped kids at the Beacon Club, and we may be disturbing/upsetting them. I hope not. That's not for us to judge. Perhaps it's for a psychologist but even more it's for the youth leaders and the kids to judge and as long as they invite us back, I assume we're doing all right.

MPB: When you were with *Interaction*, wasn't it more into

encounter groups?

BM: *Interaction* developed and marketed a thing called the *Interaction* game method which is really a collection of games, mostly children's, that are taught as a method of working with small groups. There is nothing new about these games and we all use them regularly, but without any mystique. Say I had forty kids and we couldn't set anything up as they were all running around, I would start by saying 'Right, everyone in a circle' and we would do rhythm patterns, touch your neighbour, piggy-in-the-middle, games to keep interest up and involve everyone and appropriate to the age group. A simple game like tag for four-year-olds is just touch and run away. But if I introduce a psychological element, like 'touch the person you're most attracted to in the group' thirteen-year-old girls find it a fascinating game. By changing the content but not the form, you can make it interesting for any age. We don't use games for clinical psychological reasons, not to be regenerative, or help people, but because it helps *us* to get the kids interested, to enjoy themselves, pass the time, but not because of some remedial result.

MPB: What are the difficulties?

Graham White (another BC worker): There aren't any except the stress and strain on us personally, and raising capital and finance.

BM: At a philosophical level, after the four years we've been here, I think Islington's an unhappier place now than it was four years ago, a worse place to live in for most people. We went up to Peterborough to look at their Community Development Department, and it's the only buoyant group of statutory officials I've seen. I think it's because Peterborough's becoming a bit better place to live in every day. I think the reason Islington's becoming a shittier place is that there are hundreds of forces that are beyond us and you get really pissed off having to live and work in a place that's sinking.

MPB: That's always worried me about community work – you work with the locals to get a playgroup going, and the GLC stick a motorway through the district while you're doing it. How can you affect the political thing?

BM: Because of our closeness to the ground, we are listened to and politicians who are pretty ignorant of what's happening are happy to be approached by us; especially as, by and large, they're kept in ignorance by their officers who don't want to tell them about their mistakes and failures. Nearly all the team know some councillors and we're always talking to them. Occasionally we write letters and reports. We turn up at council meetings, and we put local groups in the picture.

GW: What we'll do is stimulate and support groups that are going to deal with larger problems. That's happening at this very moment in some areas.

BM: The GLC and local authorities are in such disarray that a well-mounted scheme, whether it's good or bad, can be effective.

GW: We were tangentially involved in the Piccadilly campaign, which seemingly had no chance when it started. It was going right in the face of Westminster Council and the GLC who had a well thought out plan at an advanced stage. Yet, they've been successfully held up for four or five years now.

BM: That's happened hundreds of times. The council had decided to demolish totally the Charters Road area, and all the councillors were accepting this, even if some of them only tacitly. It seemed to be a dead issue. People who lived there called a meeting or two; borrowed our loud-hailers, and the bus to move all the old people to meetings about six times; did all their printing here; they wrote to the Department of the Environment; they called a special meeting of the council; and two weeks ago, they got the council to reverse the decision. It was entirely due to the local campaign.

MPB: So why so pessimistic?

BM: I'm not pessimistic about the role of the BC. I think we've found a way of working, an attitude to the community that is as near as dammit perfect. But we're seven people with a grant of £20,000 and for every Charters Road, there are 500 Charters Roads on which we have no influence. Partly because the residents don't get it together, but mainly because the issues are too big. The traffic thing – it's becoming a nightmare to live in many streets in Islington. The schools – I get really depressed personally. I want to take my kids out of this borough, but I don't want to send them to private schools. I'm really worried as a father and that's true of hundreds of parents in Islington. The (political) system's out of control. I think most politicians and officers would admit it. It's pretty good chaos. They're not even able to organize their priorities. It's too easy to say to a councillor 'You've got your priorities all wrong.' He doesn't even know what his priorities are any more.

It's too easy to say to an officer 'You're inefficient' but you should look at the amount of stupid, fucking bureaucracy he has to cope with.

MPB: What did Graham mean about personal stress?

BM: You should ask him. The BC is all-consuming of people's time. Most probably we work a hundred hour week and when you get asked to do something on a Sunday evening that's important, you just can't turn it down. It's very demanding but that true of most community work. Also, we believe we should be paid somewhere near the rate of the people we're working with, so we deliberately pay ourselves relatively little. Compared to local authority workers, the discrepancy's outrageous.

Note McAlister's strong denial of mental health aims. Two likely reasons for this are that it would limit the range of the BC's work, and also change the BC's relationship with the community.

The BC's clarity of aims and efficiency of functioning were impressive. Certain other features of the BC are relevant to an understanding of what factors contribute to effective applied psychology:

(1) There is very strong cohesion. Most of the BC live communally in a short-life property and so obviously have a lot of informal social contact with each other. They have a wide range of interests, so that although they work long hours, their work isn't their only source of ego-gratification. The BC was fiercely egalitarian, and would confront any member they felt was ego-tripping (a reaction to *Interaction*?).

(2) They have a highly developed set of skills to offer, but are careful to avoid a prima donna role. As Graham White said 'One of the problems is that, when we roll up to a playground, for example, either the youth leader feels he's going to look less competent than us, or he feels "great, they're quite able to manage the session without me", and slopes off to the boozer. So it's important you don't roll up banging a big drum but keep a low profile.'

(3) Most crucially, they have a very good base to influence the well-being of community groups. A resource centre is at one level politically neutral. Yet because they have so many resources to offer, most groups will want to use them. These they can advise more objectively than a community worker working with only one group as they don't have all their eggs

116

in one basket. Thus, the problem of the groups becoming dependent on them is less likely to arise.

I wondered how the BC could develop further, especially as some of the staff were feeling it was time for them to move on. One aim is to get premises in the main street (Holloway Road; at the moment, they're in a side turning) where they would have a coffee bar and bookshop in addition to their existing resources. This of course would greatly increase their running costs and the size of their operations. I fear it might be a memorial to the BC's founders and a millstone to those who follow.

Community work 3: Centreprise, Hackney

A community resource agency that does have a coffee bar and bookshop is Centreprise, situated in a main road in Hackney. The short excerpt below is from a conversation with John Rowley. A psychology graduate, he spent some time in management consultancy before joining Centreprise. He runs the bookshop and is currently working on two projects: the preparation of a guide to the health and welfare services in Hackney; and an adult literacy scheme (in conjunction with a local college of further education.)

JR: Do I use my psychology training? No. Occasionally, I use the group dynamic stuff I learnt at business school to try and understand what's going on in groups I'm involved in.

The coffee bar's important as, besides providing reasonably priced food and drink, it's a place where people can come and get information from the notice-boards and see what's going on without any commitment to get involved. For example, no one's going to walk through a door marked 'literacy class' but they will come if they are coming in to have a coffee with their (volunteer) tutor and then moving upstairs for a session.

We have three meeting rooms and they're used most evenings. There aren't many places where you can hold meetings in Hackney, especially political ones, which church halls, etc. won't accept. They could use library rooms but they're not conducive to a good group feeling, and just as you get going, along comes the caretaker and turfs you out.

The Publishing Project publishes work by local people, all of whom have been people with no experience of further

117

education. These books are bought by local people because they know or have heard of the author, and what's in them are experiences that are part of their lives too. One book of poetry by a West Indian teenager has had tremendous local sales. Last year, we sold 20,000 books produced by the Publishing Project. Books are thought of as things that are very difficult to produce and need a host of middlemen and professionals to edit, print, distribute, advertise, etc., so naturally people see no possibility of involving themselves in such activities. What the Publishing Project is doing is breaking down this barrier – it's offering technology so that Hackney people, schoolchildren can write something and can get it produced easily, quickly and cheaply. (We try to involve them in the publishing process so they see there's no mystery and learn the skills.) When a mother sees a book of poems, which is nicely produced, and the book she's holding in her hand has got a poem written by her Susan, that's going to change what books mean to her. She sees that books don't have to be things the middle class read and discuss, but can be part of her life. And the same thinking is behind our silkscreen and photographic workshop. He went on to describe other activities carried out by Centreprise's nine full-time workers, such as an advice centre, community work, etc.

MPB: What are the difficulties involved in such work?

JR: One thing that does bother me is the relationship between the community worker and the local residents. If you think you're going to raise their level of consciousness, you've got to realize that's light years away. Sure, they could apply for their own funding and I'm sure the Gulbenkian would be only too pleased to hear from them. But then they'd have to get an accountant, write up proposals, progress reports, etc. – do the whole *bourgeois* trip. Look, these community efforts aren't for the working class. They're for the middle class person – often upper class with their own money – who want to experiment with their own ideas. They've got nothing in common with the working class. They don't think like them, don't have the same interests, and if they choose to live in a slum, they know *they* can up and off tomorrow. They seem to need to work in working-class areas, and if what they do is liked by the locals, then the locals can use it; but they're not offering the working class choices. They're not saying 'what do *you* want *us* to do?' They're providing the resources *they* think

118

the working class need, not providing genuine choices for the locals to decide between.

And, of course, the same applies to mental health services to an even greater extent. One of the refreshing things about community work is, because the role is relatively new, the workers are much more ready to question what they are and should be doing, than is the case in more traditional fields.

The implications of community work for mental health are well put by Reiff (1966):

—disturbed middle-class patients see themselves as *victims of their own selves*. Low-income people, on the other hand, ... live in a world of limited or no opportunities. They see themselves as *victims of circumstances*. Self-actualisation under these conditions is meaningless to them. Before they can become interested in self-actualisation, they have to believe that they can play a role in determining what happens to them. Thus, *self*-determination rather than self-actualisation is a more realistic and more meaningful goal for them.

One may question whether the middle classes really do have the ability to change their circumstances, but one reason they feel they do is that they have access to (and control over) technological and information resources; and it is these that the members of a working class community need to improve their sense of well-being and control far more than additional mental health professionals.

Community work 4: The People's Aid and Action Centre, Battersea

The People's Aid and Action Centre (PAAC) is 'an experimental project attempting to provide a skilled counselling service in the context of a neighbourhood action centre.' It was set up in 1973 by Julian Lousada, a psychiatric social worker, and Sue Holland, who is a Tavistock-trained clinical psychologist and psychotherapist. Sited in large, run-down premises, it faces onto 'a busy shopping street'. It has suffered from lack of funds, and at the time of the interview, had only one full-time worker – Sue Holland.

MPB: Let's start with your relation to community groups.

SH: We leave it mostly to groups to come in and ask if they

can use the place. So we have the Claimants' Union (CU) and a squatters' group who run a rent-collection and information centre in the evenings; there are some music groups, who use the cellar; and various groups come and go; for example a group of parents with mentally handicapped kids are setting up a self-help group here.

The counselling bit is that if they want us to come in, we will. One or two of the CU and the squatters, after they'd been here some time, have come and asked if they can have help for instance with some marital problems. We've done some co-therapy (two therapists) with couples, mostly from the Women's Aid Centre (for battered wives) (Pizzey, 1974). Women have gone there but they also want to see if they can make a go of it with their men. (Obviously, it's better if the co-therapists are of different sex. That's why I'm keen that the second worker, we're advertising for, is a man. Also, generally, men round here find it more difficult to talk over personal problems with a woman.)

So that's one way we work – as a therapeutic resource for community groups. But we also see people on an individual level; and in the process of giving them one-to-one help, we try also to get them into a support group of some kind, like the CU. We've had a lot to do with the CU because, in this sort of area, the claimants' work and marital and other problems are very much connected. Their people are on social security, have housing problems, they're also often in difficulty with their kids or their men; and all these problems are very interlinked.

MPB: So it's a two-way thing. Isn't the link hard to forge?

SH: Yes, we really are fighting to get people to accept the idea and use us. People involved in social action certainly are very suspicious of any attempt to help with individual problems, but I think, through working with us, some people are beginning to see that *they can be* linked.

I'll give you an example. One of the CU people said they were very stuck with one of their people, for whom they'd been fighting the SS for a long time to get compensation. She was getting very pissed off and also was seriously depressed – the doctor was saying to her that she had to go into mental hospital. She'd started fainting in the SS office, so the CU person, the woman and myself all sat down and had a very long session. They were talking about what they were trying to do, the sort of difficulties she'd got into, how frightened she was she'd have to go into mental hospital. Now I, because of my psychoanalytic basis, was taking it up in terms of what she was feeling that was making her use fainting as an escape from something, as a way of dealing with the conflict. She was having to go to the SS where she'd sometimes sit in a queue all day and then be told when she got to the window 'No, we can't do it today', and she wouldn't say anything. So I was working at that level with her – that she found fainting, or even going to mental hospital, a solution, and then she said how she'd been brought up to be 'a good girl'. It was like that in Jamaica, that she mustn't lose her temper, etc. It made a lot of sense and recently she's said she's felt a lot better, has had no recurrences of fainting. They've won the case and now she wants to help set up a women's group for women in similar circumstances – their men have left them, they've got kids and can't get jobs because there are no nurseries. They really want to use themselves more, rather than sitting around at home stewing in their own anger.

Psychoanalytically, I very much link anger and depression as two faces and in our society, women tend to use depression when really they're very angry but they need to liberate their energies to actually change the world, not just themselves; but they've got to change themselves *as well* as the world. You can't just do the social thing in isolation.

MPB: So do you see yourself as freeing the energy for political things?

SH: I see any transformation of a shitty situation as a political thing, but maybe 'political' is too grand a word for it because people tend to misunderstand that and see politics as being about politicians.

MPB: How've you changed your psychoanalytic concepts?

SH: I don't think psychoanalysis is by definition anti-action. It's become that because of the way it's been used and the sort of interests it's been used for. I think the problem in psychoanalysis is precisely that it hasn't dealt with how impulses, which it talks a lot about, are *transformed* into actions. It's no good talking about having impulses unless you talk about what the impulses are going into, which usually means human relationships, which means social relationships. At the Tavistock (Clinic, London), they tend to leave it simply in the mind, at the head level, and not to actually go into how that can affect behaviour and action. To be fair to the Tavistock, it had a very radical history. There were people like Fairbairn, (1952) the creator of object relations theory, coming out of the army after the War, who began to look at the need for people to change things and change their social lives, not just their intrapsychic thing. Unfortunately, the place has been taken over by the Kleinians, who, with their emphasis on instinctual agression which is externalized, are very reactionary.

MPB: How do you advertise the counselling service?

SH: We're still really stuck as to how we should advertise, because the word 'counselling' isn't understood by people. Because of our lack of cash, we never have advertised. We've tended to say this is a place where people can come and we'll try to help them with *any* problem – housing, CU, marital, any type. We haven't really solved this – how we get across to people.

MPB: Would you like to move into trying to provide alternatives to hospital here?

SH: I don't think we can be an alternative to hospitals. Where we think we're working, rather ineffectively, is preventive work to stop people going into hospital. Certainly, in this area, people are sent to hospital very quickly because they don't get any therapeutic treatment; the GPs just prescribe drugs; the social workers are totally overburdened and haven't had much training in therapy. We've got very mixed relations with social workers. On the one hand, they see us as interfering, and we *are*, because people come to us when they think social workers have got them into a mess. Others work quite closely with us. There's a couple of social workers here every Thursday running an intermediate treatment group for kids. Social workers sometimes send us people they can't help because they're not set up to do much therapy.

One thing that worries me about Social Services is that they may start encouraging self-help groups to save money and pretend it's equivalent to therapy. That will just perpetuate the present state where only the middle classes get therapy. What we're trying to show is that there's a need for counselling in areas like this, and residents have got a right to have such a service. We'd like people to come in with problems before they build up. But, in fact, we've mainly had people who are chronic problems for the SS/legal/welfare systems. So, many of the cases are people appealing to Tribunals against decisions made by these systems, and we work quite a bit with Law Centres.

They refer people to me when they want some psychological help or information, and we send people to them when we need legal advice.

One Law Centre phoned me, saying 'there's a guy here, who's in Tooting Bec. hospital, and he's very angry. First, he says they've accused him of assault, and the other thing he's angry about is that they won't let him see his wife who's on another ward.' He came here and we talked; and I wasn't really sure this was his wife and why he wasn't being allowed to see her. I phoned the psychiatrist who said 'Well, you know, he's a paranoid schizophrenic. You can't believe anything he says.' Well, I was almost put off by that but the Law Centre helped *me* by saying 'We'll fight it' and I said 'I think it's worth it, apart from this case, to show the hospital we've got our eye on them and on that psychiatrist' – I'd already got a folder on him because of people coming to me complaining about him. So they fought it and in fact they got a photocopy from the Town Hall of the marriage licence.

This sort of work ties up with the Community Health Council (CHC) which is supposed to be the grass roots voice of the Health Service. Its offices are temporarily here, much to the disgust of the Tories on it, because I'm the chairman.

MPB: I thought they forgot to issue the CHCs with dentures.

SH: They have no power in fact, and one of the reasons I'm on it is to expose that. But you also get a lot of information you couldn't possibly get any other way, and it's quite useful as a propaganda thing. Not only does it get press coverage, the hospitals have to put the CHC advert on their noticeboards, whereas you couldn't get a PAAC poster on them.

MPB: This project seems to have been slow, hard work.

SH: You could just spell out so many difficulties we've had, it's amazing we've stayed open. One of our fights was that we should get the same salary as we'd get in the NHS. In fact, I get £1,000 less and we had such difficulty getting a second salary, Julian went off to work for Islington, although he's still involved on a voluntary basis. We've had people in doing voluntary work. Fortunately, John's here all the time, running the Food Coop for OAPs and people on social security, so he sees people if I'm tied up (John, a war disabled pensioner, was helped by PAAC and then stayed on to help). We ask people to come back but they rarely do, because they come in on impulse.

123

I think we need part-time workers and definitely a secretary. But now, at last, we're a going concern and we've no financial worries for a year. Battersea Council's giving us £6,000 to pay for two workers and expenses. (The Mental Health Trust who've been paying me up to now will stop.) So now we can really get down to the experimental project – to develop a methodology of doing individual counselling which relates to social action. We haven't got one yet. There's Freud on one side, Marx on the other. There's got to be a link.

I bade my farewells to Sue, John, and a social worker, who'd come about the second post. As I drove back along the river, I videoed the scene in my mind. We'd been sitting at a table in the middle of the large bare shop front. On one wall, there were copies of left-wing papers, the local community news sheet, and a poster urging one to help fight the developers taking over Battersea. On the other wall, was a MIND poster informing us that 'every two minutes another person needs help from mental hospital services' with a picture of a bloke who looked like he'd just got off a rush-hour tube. Behind me sat John, smoking his pipe, seemingly oblivious to our conversation, guarding the Food Coop's cart with its spuds and onions. In front of me were a psychologist striving to combine counselling and community action, and a social worker gaining little satisfaction from her work.

It was in no way a conclusion. It would do as a summing up.

5
Ticket to ride: the future

In this final chapter, I want to consider the future of community psychology ideas in this country, and the type of training that would be most suitable.

Community psychology as a theory, and as an approach

Two things are clear: (1) *a formal theory* of 'community psychology' is light years away, if not unachievable, and (2) the community psychology *approach* has a great deal to offer British applied psychology.

Some of the reasons that 'community psychology' cannot be considered a unified theory or practice are: (1) in the past when two sciences have fruitfully contributed to a new discipline, at least one of them has had a clearly defined set of axiomatic statements, which provides the basis for translation into the language of the other science, e.g. physical chemistry, molecular biology (Kuhn, 1970). This is not the case with either psychology or sociology, so how can the offspring of these two obese adolescents be any healthier?

(2) The term 'community psychologist' conceals two different groups of workers – the psychologists applying their techniques to groups in the community; and community workers, whose training in psychology now forms a very small part of their repertoire of skills. These two groups have different priorities of concern, and different skills. Thus, I cannot imagine the

Islington BC would get much joy out of applying behavioural methods in children's homes, nor the Birmingham workers feeling particularly happy driving a playbus around. Whilst one should be *aware* of the various levels at which one might tackle a problem, one cannot profitably *work* at the levels simultaneously without inevitably failing to maximize one's utility at any level.

(3) Community psychology implies a political role for the psychologist. Political skills are not on psychology courses, nor is there much likelihood that they will be. Without such skills, as Caplan once remarked, 'any third rate politician will run rings round a psychologist.'

(4) There is a role confusion. The psychologist is esentially a technician, however independent and however carefully he considers the ethical implications of his contracts. If he wishes to influence political processes beyond providing information concerning the field of his speciality, he is free to do so – but he is doing so in his role as a citizen. Community psychologists seem to want to get paid for being citizens. As Hume pointed out in 1736, one cannot logically argue from an 'is' to an 'ought' (the Naturalistic Fallacy). However shocking conditions are, it is not a scientific but an *ethical* decision that something be done about them, and to confuse the two roles is to further weaken the democratic process.

(5) There is an overselling of psychologists' skills, based on the logical fallacy of the excluded middle. Bad housing has a clear if complex relationship with mental illness. Because psychologists can claim some expertise in helping the mentally ill, it in no way follows they are experts about planning and housing. For that, we need better architects and town planners.

One could go on. Having stripped away the pretensions, the skills and attitudes of community psychologists are of considerable value, since (1) they have a greater awareness, which leads to a more effective use of existing skills.

(2) Since certain client groups have been traditionally neglected by applied psychology and others not considered within its ambit at all, this has led to a wider application of psychological skills.

(3) This is related to a greater sense of responsibility to the clients and consumers of psychological services. It is to them, not to our bosses or profession that we are finally accountable.

(4) Working in new areas has led to the development of new

techniques and approaches.

(5) They have realized the importance of influencing organizations, and not just individuals. They have therefore developed a greater organizational awareness and sophistication.

(6) A related point: they have a greater ability to handle and create change, since the demands placed upon the welfare establishments are continually changing, while in community groups, the situation is even more fluid. (Sarason, 1967.)

(7) 'Change typically involves risk and fear. Any significant change in human organization involves rearrangement of patterns of power, association, status, skills and values.' (Bennis, in Cook, 1970.) Thus, there is more emphasis on group dynamics. At the field level, the academic model of competitive individualism is inappropriate, while a psychologist who can work cooperatively without sacrificing his individuality is likely to be more effective.

These points have been illustrated earlier and therefore I shall not elaborate on them. Perhaps they can be summarized by saying a community psychology approach would help applied psychology to become a more responsible and effective profession.

Training

If community psychology ideas are to enter psychologists' thinking, this will have to start at undergraduate level. Current psychology courses are essentially geared to the creation of academic psychologists, who are very poorly trained to tackle significant problems due to their need to be 'scientifically respectable' (Bender, 1974). Not only does this grossly devalue the contribution psychology *could* make, by claiming an importance it does not at present merit, psychology then has to defend this delusion. This leaves it in a very poor position to criticize the practices of other professions, or existing services. Clearly, if students are to gain the skills and attributes outlined previously, the selection and training of psychology students will need to be radically changed.

Undergraduate training

Students should be selected who have worked in jobs that demonstrate their interest in theoretical or applied psychology;

at the least, they should have worked in a variety of jobs that would give them experiences which they could use as one way of assessing the utility of psychological theories. At the moment, coming straight from school, students are too immature to criticize effectively psychological ideas or practices.

Three essential attributes that the course should teach are: (1) an awareness that psychology is only one way of construing man's behaviour among many, equally valid ways; (2) a high commitment to the application of psychological ideas and techniques to all persons who might benefit from them; and (3) a highly developed critical ability regarding the quality of their own and others' work.

(1) Understanding the strengths and limitations of psychological ideas when analysing behaviour could perhaps be best achieved by centring the course around the theme of 'the development of the person in society', development being seen as a continuous process from birth to death. The core aspects of psychology, such as memory, perception, learning, would then be seen as relatively invariant across cultures, whereas much of personality and social psychology would be seen as highly variable across cultures. This variance would need explaining in terms of historical, sociological, and anthropological concepts. Thus, such an approach retains the essence of psychology – the study of the *individual's* experience – while placing it firmly in a social and cultural context.

(2) The practical utility of psychological theories could be shown by explaining the implications (if any) of the concepts being taught to real life situations, and by placements outside the university. (This, of course, is already being done in some universities, such as Aston, Brunel, UWIST.) This would lessen the likelihood of the psychology degree being the oddly unreal experience, divorced from the everyday world, it is felt to be by many students. For example, as undergraduates, we had a seminar on Laing – were his ideas right or wrong? (see F3). *Not one student in that room had actually seen, let alone spoken to, a schizophrenic.*

(3) Ability to assess one's own and other people's work is part of the scientific method. The scientific method is basically a set of attitudes, a way of relating to others, since it includes *communism* ('the substantive findings of science are a product of social collaboration and are assigned to the community'), *disinterestedness* (scientific findings must be independent of per-

sonal gain) and *organized scepticism* (suspension of judgement, until the necessary data are at hand, independent of institutional opinions as to what is the case), etc. (Merton, 1967, in Barnes, 1972). One way for students to internalize the scientific method would be for them to develop a topic *of interest to themselves* into a researchable project. This would show the strengths of research methodology (to come up with objective, fairly clear-cut answers) and the weaknesses (its inability to answer philosophical or moral questions).

Postgraduate

There should be a common course for clinical, educational, and occupational psychologists. The present separate training courses decrease the number of dimensions on which these various sub-specialists can think and act. A competent applied psychologist should be able to investigate, analyse, and operate within any institution where he has relevant skills; and the various sub-specialists vary relatively little in the skills they use.

Students should be selected who have shown through their work a commitment to the betterment of social conditions. Little account should be taken of academic grades at under-graduate level as they correlate *negatively* with clinical ability (Carkhuff, 1969). Certainly, no student should be accepted who has not spent some time outside the educational system.

Turning to *training*, research methods should be taught with regard to the context in which they'll be applied. Most applied psychologists are fieldworkers, not research workers, and will only be able to utilize simple research designs. To train them as research workers and teach them complicated statistical designs is a sad reminder of applied psychology's obeisance to the 'higher' status of academic psychology.

If statistical sophistication is less necessary, their research methods need to be as ingenious and as flexible as possible. Thus, they should be discouraged from undertaking projects of the 'find twenty deviants and bash them with five tests' variety, which will not develop either of these qualities, but which all too often are encouraged on current clinical courses. Theses should relate to ongoing fieldwork, either their own, or preferably that of a practising psychologist. It is often difficult for an applied psychologist to fit his fieldwork into a research design, because it reduces his flexibility of action. However, this need not stop an outside researcher (the student) looking at a project's utility. I would like to see a clearing-house whereby field psychologists inform students of their ongoing projects, and the students select one to investigate its efficacy. In such projects, the student would have to tackle the difficulties of defining problems and goals in ways amenable to measurement, setting time limits and targets, getting decent records kept, etc., which would increase his organizational awareness. It is likely he would gain experience in using the large number of simple and useful methodologies now available, such as time-sampling (see C1), unobtrusive measures, content analysis, survey techniques, and so on. Through such placements, then, the student would get a thorough grounding in assessment and monitoring techniques, which are essential to sound programme development.

As regards *therapy*, students should, after training, achieve adequate standards on the dimensions of accurate empathy, non-possessive warmth and genuineness, since Truax and Carkhuff (1967) and others have shown that therapists who do not exhibit such qualities are psychonoxious – i.e. harm their clients. A responsible profession does not allow such therapists loose. In addition, a great lack in contemporary courses is that the student is not taught how to structure and handle an interview, whether it be exploratory or therapeutic. Since such a skill is necessary when communicating with both staff and clients, it is essential that the students become competent interviewers.

In order to understand the context in which his therapeutic efforts will occur, it would be useful for students to work for a period in a patient-management role – as a nursing assistant, or residential or day care staff (Rosenhan, 1973).

Besides research and therapeutic skills, two other key concepts on the course should be *role awareness* and *institutional awareness*. By role awareness, I mean a coherent understanding of the role of the professional, especially the psychologist, in society and the relevant literature is that of the sociology of science (Merton, 1973; Barnes, 1972); by institutional awareness, I mean comprehending how bureaucracies work both at a formal and informal level – the field of organizational psychology (Bennis *et al.*, 1970). In addition to theoretical understanding, these awarenesses need to be developed out of fieldwork placements. Instead of the very restricted range of placements currently offered to applied students, these should be in a wide variety of settings, especially outside the large, established institutions. They might include doss-houses, anti-psychiatry hostels, adventure playgrounds, for example. Their aim would be to provide the student with a breadth of experience and understanding of institutions, and of his role within them.

One attribute that would hopefully be developed by such placements would be the ability to assess situations quickly and the payoff of various courses of actions. Clinical courses are uninterested in situations where research is not likely to be undertaken. However, there are many situations in any applied psychologist's work, where however much he would like to stop and gather empirical data, he has neither the time nor the opportunity to do so and where he has to make important decisions, using whatever information is available. Students need some training on how to tackle such situations. How such skills can be developed is problematic but the use of simulation techniques might be one way (see E3).

This skill is related to two final areas. The student needs a sound concept of *group dynamics*, and the ability to act effectively within groups. Here, the use of videotape and social skills training might well be helpful. Similar methods could be used to develop the student's *ability to transmit skills* efficiently, both formally and informally.

So far we have dealt with skills that would be taught to all the students – research and therapy skills, role and institutional awareness, the ability to handle change, and transmit skills. Clearly, there would also have to be modules for the sub-specialisms. Probably, the most useful split would be child/adult. Whilst the modules would provide greater theoretical depth, their main function would be to teach the legislation and traditions of institutions associated with the care of children, or of adults. It is the knowledge of the bureaucratic options open to one in a given institution that is vital to successful work. As Colin Critchley put it 'You can learn all the skills needed for this game in twelve months. It takes you years to understand and manipulate the bureaucracy effectively.'

Overall, then, the function of the course would be to give the student a thorough grounding in existing skills, in the additional ones needed to work effectively in a variety of institutions, and a focused commitment.

The most important factor in the development of community psychology in Britain is research work that will put it on a sound empirical footing. It is often argued that applied psychology develops from theoretical research, and an example given is behaviour therapy, which developed from learning theory. However, I would suggest that research efforts concerning the questions community psychology is asking will produce areas of inquiry that will be more fruitful to psychology than those posed by laboratory studies. Such areas as family and organizational dynamics could provide valuable data for the further development of personality theory and social psychology (see D3 and B2). Certainly, efforts should be switched from the unprofitable areas of individual pathology and the study of patients with no regard for their social context, and still linked to the medical model (Bedford and Foulds, 1975), which occupies the bulk of clinical psychological research at the present time. There need to be far more studies into the efficacy of preventive programmes; into the long-term effects of skills-transmission, especially to New Careerists and para-professionals; multivariable studies on the effects of community programmes. Another and very important group of studies that needs further development is that relating types of institutional organization to the quality of care they provide (Wing and Brown, 1970; King, *et al.*, 1971). The development of scales measuring ward activity, child management, linguistic stimulation, family dysfunction, etc., allow the psychologist to measure basic variables in institutional life and relate them to the development and well-being of inmates (and have powerful policy implications). These lines of research are only some of the possibilities and are promising starts to strengthening the empirical foundations of community psychology. It is an area that could produce tremendous dividends for psychology, both at the applied and theoretical levels, but its development will be dependent, unfortunately, on the number of research workers who are 'participants rather than critics' (Carkhuff, 1969).

I outlined above what I consider the necessary attributes for effective psychology in the community, and a possible training. I have no illusions that any such changes will happen – British psychology is far too busy consolidating itself to become open and self-critical. In the clinical field, this may be due to emigration. Whatever the reason, the season ticket holders will journey on. Clinical psychology used to be polarized between the psychoanalysts and the behaviourists. Psychoanalysis is now too discredited to command much loyalty, and the soft radical wing has been inherited by those interested in encounter groups, gestalt, body awareness, etc. As befits their heritage, these methods, which have little empirical validity (Campbell and Dunnette, 1968) are only of use to persons with no gross personality difficulties; moreover their fascination with the state of their feelings limits the utility to community groups whose problems relate to larger issues and whose pressing needs require a less introspective approach. The hard-liners, the behavioural analysts will expand in number as they have an efficient, if limited, product to sell (see A3); but their methods are most appropriate to closed institutions, where the 'therapeutic agents' have real control over the inmates' lives (see F1, F8). Behavioural theory is very impoverished in awareness of multiple perspectives, its language unsubtle and limited in its emotional range, and its practitioners more committed to the development of their techniques than the well-being of the community. While as a set of techniques it has much to offer in the field of prevention, as an approach it cannot be used for the planning of services or as a basis for wide-range attempts to alleviate unnecessary psychic distress.

Any new methods coming out of community psychology, which are shown to have validity, will of course slowly be absorbed into the mainstream. What will be missing, unless selection and training change radically, will be a reorientation of psychology into an actively caring, reaching out profession, not afraid to be out of goose-step with the other mental health professions. The need for such a reorientation is likely to increase if the polarization of attitudes that seems to be occurring in our society continues. Applied psychologists need to be seen as standing clearly for client choice and the right of *every* person to decent mental health services. The opportunities are there, in the welfare services, in the community groups and voluntary bodies, for psychologists who have the flexibility to exploit them; but they won't get much support and they'll have to retrain themselves.

What hope there is, then, must lie with individuals coming through the system, who, while rejecting the pretensions of our tragi-comic profession, can discriminate the useful theory and practice, and go beyond it. What impact psychology makes in the community will depend on the incremental efforts of such people. What a psychologist does depends on his priorities, his values. There are costs and difficulties in stepping out of the well-tried and ineffective ways of working. It has to be an individual choice, made by each psychologist, each psychology student. Your choice.

Travel light.

Further Reading

Chapter 1
Historical
Arthur, R. J. (1971) *An Introduction to Social Psychiatry.* Harmondsworth: Penguin.
Shakow, D. (1969) *Clinical Psychology as Science and Profession.* Chicago: Aldine.
Clinical psychology
Foulds, G. A. (1965) *Personality and Personal Illness.* London: Tavistock.
Family studies
Handel, G. (ed.) (1968) *The Psychological Interior of the Family.* London: George Allen and Unwin.
Sociology of mental illness
Weinberg, S. K. (ed.) (1967) *The Sociology of Mental Disorders.* London: Staple Press.
Community psychology
Adelson, D. and Kalis, B. L. (eds) (1970) *Community Psychology and Mental Health.* Scranton: Chandler.
Bindman, A. J. and Spiegel, A. D. (eds) (1969) *Perspectives in Community Mental Health.* Chicago: Aldine.
Carter, J. W. (ed.) (1968) *Research Contributions from Psychology to Community Mental Health.* New York: Behavioural Publications.
Cook, P. E. (ed.) (1970) *Community Psychology and Community Mental Health.* San Francisco: Holden-Day.
Community Psychiatry
Susser, M. (1968) *Community Psychiatry.* New York: Random House.

Social Psychiatry
Jones, M. (1953) *The Therapeutic Community.* New York: Basic Books.

Chapter 2
Methods of intervention
Hornstein, H., Bunker, B., Burke, W., Gindes, M. and Lewicki, R. (1971) *Social Intervention.* New York: The Free Press.

Chapter 3
The training of nurse therapists
Carkhuff, R. R. (1969) *Helping and Human Relations* (2 vols). New York: Holt, Rinehart and Winston.

Hallam, R. S. (1975) The training of nurses as therapists: outcome and implications. *Bulletin of the British Psychological Society* 28: 331–6.

Newham
Bender, M. P. (1972) The role of a community psychologist. *Bulletin of the British Psychological Society* 25: 211–18.

Hawks, D. V. (ed.) (1976) *Psychology in the Community.* London: Angus and Robertson.

Birmingham
Tharp, R. G. and Wetzel, R. J. (1969) *Behaviour Modification in the Natural Environment.* New York: Academic Press.

Services for the handicapped
Clarke, A. M. and Clarke, A. D. B. (eds) (1974) *Mental Deficiency: The Changing Outlook.* London: Methuen.

Tizard, J. (1972) Research in services for the mentally handicapped: science and policy issues. *British Journal of Mental Subnormality* 18: 1–12.

Child Guidance
Tizard, J. (1973) Maladjusted children and the child guidance service. *London Education Review* 2: 22–37.

Residential care
King, R. D., Raynes, N. V. and Tizard, J. (1971) *Patterns of Residential Care.* London: Routledge and Kegan Paul.

Wing, J. K. and Brown, G. W. (1970) *Institutionalism and Schizophrenia.* Cambridge: Cambridge University Press.

Preventive psychiatry
Caplan, G. (1964) *Principles of Preventive Psychiatry.* London: Tavistock.

Parkes, C. M. (1971) Psycho-social transitions: a field for study. *Social Science and Medicine* 5: 101–15.

Bereavement
Parkes, C. M. (1975) *Bereavement.* Harmondsworth: Penguin.

New Careers

Guerney, B. G. Jr (ed.) (1969) *Psychotherapeutic Agents: New Roles for Nonprofessionals, Parents and Teachers.* New York: Holt, Rinehart and Winston.

Hinton, N. (Jan. 1973) Offenders as social workers. *Social Work Today 3*: 9–11. (See also Castles and Briggs in the same volume.)

Pearl, A. and Reissman, F. (1965) *New Careers for the Poor.* New York: The Free Press (available from Macmillan, London).

Community work

Brager, G. and Sprecht, H. (1973) *Community Organizing.* New York: Columbia University Press.

Jones, D. and Mayo, M. (eds) (1974) *Community Work: One.* London: Routledge and Kegan Paul.

Marris, P. and Rein, M. (1974) *Dilemmas of Social Reform.* Harmondsworth: Penguin.

Radical Therapist Collective (1974) *The Radical Therapist.* Harmondsworth, Penguin.

Chapter 4

Training

Bender, M. P. (1974) Psychology: industry and/or scientific craft. *Bulletin of the British Psychological Society 27*: 107–15.

Tizard, J. (1974) The upbringing of other people's children: implications of research and for research. *Journal of Child Psychology and Psychiatry 15*: 161–73.

Sociology of science

Barnes, B. (ed.) (1972) *The Sociology of Science.* Harmondsworth: Penguin.

Kuhn, T. S. (1970) *The Structure of Scientific Revolutions* (2nd edn). Chicago: University of Chicago Press.

Merton, R. K. (1973) *The Sociology of Science.* Chicago: The University of Chicago.

Organizational psychology

Bennis, W. G., Benne, K. D. and Chin, R. (eds) (1970) *The Planning of Change* (2nd edn). New York: Holt, Rinehart and Winston.

Katz, E. and Danet, B. (eds) (1973) *Bureaucracy and the Public.* New York: Basic Books.

Tizard, J., Sinclair, I. and Clarke, R. V. G. (eds) (1975) *Varieties of Residential Experience.* London: Routledge & Kegan Paul.

References and Name Index

The numbers in italics after each entry refer to page numbers within this book.

Adelson, D. and Kalis, B. L. (eds) (1970) *Community Psychology and Mental Health.* Scranton: Chandler. *31, 34, 35, 36, 37*

Albee, G. W. (1959) *Mental Health Manpower Trends.* New York: Basic Books. *21*

Albee, G. W. (1968) Conceptual models and manpower requirements in psychology. *American Psychologist 23*: 317–20. *21*

Albee, G. W. (1970) The uncertain future of clinical psychology. *American Psychologist 25*: 1071–80. *32*

Alinsky, S. (1971) *Rules for Radicals.* New York: Random House. *33, 53*

Anthony, W. A., Buell, G. J., Sharratt, S. and Althoff, M. E. (1972) Efficacy of psychiatric rehabilitation. *Psychological Bulletin 78*: 447–56. *19*

Arthur, R. J. (1971) *An Introduction to Social Psychiatry.* Harmondsworth: Penguin. *16, 80*

Barnes, B. (ed.) (1972) *The Sociology of Science.* Harmondsworth: Penguin. *129, 130*

Bateson, G., Jackson, D. D., Haley, J. and Weakland, J. (1956) Toward a theory of schizophrenia. *Behavioral Science 1*: 251–64. *22–3*

Bedford, A. and Foulds, G. A. (1975) Humpty Dumpty and psychiatric diagnosis. *Bulletin of the British Psychological Society 28*: 208–11. *132*

Beech, H. R. (1969) *Changing Man's Behaviour.* Harmondsworth: Penguin. *28*

Bender, M. P. (1974) Psychology: industry and/or scientific craft? *Bulletin of the British Psychological Society 27*: 107–15. *127*

Bennett, C. C. (1965) Community psychology: impressions of the Boston Conference on the education of psychologists for community mental health. *American Psychologist 20*: 832–5. *62*

Bennis, W. G., Benne, K. D. and Chin, R. (eds) (1970) *The Planning of Change* (2nd edn) New York: Holt, Rinehart & Winston. *33, 130*

Berger, M. (1975) Clinical psychology services for children. *Bulletin of the British Psychological Society 28*: 102–7. *84*

Bernstein, B. (1973) *Class, Codes and Control*. London: Paladin. *12*

Bowlby, J. (1953) *Child Care and the Growth of Love*. Harmondsworth: Penguin. *90*

Boyers, R. and Orrill, R. (eds) (1972) *Laing and Anti-psychiatry*. Harmondsworth: Penguin. *23*

Brager, G. and Specht, H. (1973) *Community Organising*. New York: Columbia University Press. *101*

Butcher, H. J. (1968) *Human Intelligence: Its Nature and Assessment*. London: Methuen. *25*

Caine, T. M. and Smail, D. J. (1969) *Science, Faith and the Therapeutic Personality*. London: University of London Press. *18*

Campbell, J. P. and Dunnette, M. D. (1968) Effectiveness of T-group experiences in managerial training and development. *Psychological Bulletin 70*: 73–104. *133*

Canter, D. (1974) Empirical research in environmental psychology. *Bulletin of the British Psychological Society 27*: 31–7. *35*

Caplan, G. (1961) *An Approach to Community Mental Health*. London: Tavistock. *27*

Caplan, G. (1964) *Principles of Preventive Psychiatry*. London: Tavistock. *34, 88–90, 106*

Caplan, G. (1970) *The Theory and Practice of Mental Health Consultation*. London: Tavistock. *35, 90, 94*

Carkhuff, R. R. (1969) *Helping and Human Relations*. New York: Holt, Rinehart & Winston, 2 vols. *36, 129, 132*

Carter, J. W. (ed.) (1968) *Research Contributions from Psychology to Community Mental Health*. New York: Behavioural Publications. *34*

Clarke, A. M. & Clarke, A. D. B. (eds) (1974) *Mental Deficiency: The Changing Outlook*. London: Methuen. *81, 87*

Cohen, S. (ed.) (1971) *Images of Deviance*. Harmondsworth: Penguin. *33*

Connery, R. H. and contributors (1968) *The Politics of Mental Health*. New York: Columbia University Press. *29, 33*

Connolly, K. and Bruner, J. S. (eds) (1974) *The Growth of Competence*. New York: Academic. *81*

Cook, P. E. (ed.) (1970) *Community Psychology and Community Mental Health*. San Francisco: Holden-Day. *13, 35, 89, 127*

Cowen, E. L., Leibowitz, E. and Leibowitz, G. (1968) Utilisation of retired people as mental health aides with children. *American Journal of Orthopsychiatry 38*: 900–9. *34, 36*

Cumming, J. and Cumming, E. (1962) *Ego and Milieu*. New York: Atherton. *24*

Ellis, A. (1953) Recent research with personality inventories. *Journal of Consulting Psychology 17*: 45–50. *21*

Eysenck, H. J. (1952) The effects of psychotherapy: an evaluation. *Journal of Consulting Psychology 16*: 319–24. *20*

Fairbairn, W. R. D. (1952) *Psycho-analytic studies of the personality*. London: Tavistock. *122*

Fairweather, G. W., Sanders, D. H., Cressler, D. L. and Maynard, H. (1969) *Community Life for the Mentally Ill*. Chicago: Aldine. *34*

Farber, B. (1960) Family organisation and crisis: Maintenance of integration in families with a severely mentally retarded child. *Monogr. Soc. Res. Child. Developm. 24*: no. 1. *79*

Foulds, G. A. (1965) *Personality and personal illness*. London: Tavistock. *16, 17*

Goffman, E. (1961) *Asylums*. Garden City, New York: Anchor. *24, 29, 33*

Grob, G. N. (1966) The state mental hospital in mid-nineteenth century America. *American Psychologist, 21*: 510–23. *16*

Guerney, B. G., jr. (ed.) (1969) *Psycho-Therapeutic Agents: New Roles for Nonprofessionals, Parents and Teachers.* New York: Holt, Rinehart & Winston. *36, 37, 99*

Haley, J. and Hoffman, L. (1967) *Techniques of Family Therapy.* New York: Basic Books. *23*

Handel, G. (ed.) (1968) *The Psychosocial Interior of the Family.* London: George Allen & Unwin. *23*

Hart, J. T. (1971) The inverse care law. *Lancet* (February 1971). *26*

Hawks, D. V. (1971) Can clinical psychology afford to treat the individual? *Bulletin of the British Psychological Society* 24: 133–5. *21*

Hawks, D. V. (ed.) (1976) *Psychology in the Community.* London: Angus and Robertson. *101*

Hinton, N. (1973) Offenders as social workers. *Social Work Today 3*: 9–11. *36, 96*

Hollingshead, A. B. and Redlich, F. C. (1958) *Social Class and Mental Illness.* New York: Wiley. *12, 24–5*

Jackson, B. (1968) *Working Class Community.* London: Routledge and Kegan Paul. *11*

Jones, A. (1974) Volunteer teaching: kith and kids. *New Psychiatry 1*: 16–18. *87*

Jones, A. (1975) Parents need facts – not just sympathy. *New Psychiatry 2*: 12–13. *87*

Jones, D. and Mayo, M. (eds) (1974) *Community Work: One.* London: Routledge and Kegan Paul. *11*

Jones, M. *et al* (1952) *Social Psychiatry.* London: Tavistock. *18*

Katz, E. and Danet, B. (eds) (1973) *Bureaucracy and the Public.* New York: Basic Books. *33*

Kear-Colwell, J. J. (1972) A study of clinical psychologists' job movements during the period 1.10.67 to 30.9.70. *Bulletin of the British Psychological Society* 25: 25–7. *46*

Kesey, K. (1962) *One flew Over the Cuckoo's Nest.* London: Picador. *24*

King, R. D., Raynes, N. V. and Tizard, J. (1971) *Patterns of Residential Care.* London: Routledge and Kegan Paul. *81, 85, 132*

Kuhn, T. S. (1970) *The Structure of Scientific Revolutions* (2nd ed.) Chicago: University of Chicago Press. *125*

Laing, R. D. (1960) *The Divided Self.* London: Tavistock; Harmondsworth: Penguin. *23*

Laing, R. D. (1967) *The Politics of Experience.* Harmondsworth: Penguin. *23, 33*

Laing, R. D. and Esterson, A. (1964) *Sanity, Madness and the Family.* London: Tavistock; Harmondsworth: Penguin. *23*

Levitt, E. E. (1957) The results of psychotherapy with children: an evaluation. *Journal of Consulting Psychology* 21: 189–96. *20*

Likorish, J. R. and Sims, C. A. (1971) How much can a clinical psychologist do? *Bulletin of the British Psychological Society* 24: 27–30. *21*

Lipset, S. M. (ed.) (1969) *Politics and the Social Sciences.* New York: Oxford University Press. *10*

London, P. (1964) *The Modes and Morals of Psychotherapy.* New York: Holt, Rinehart & Winston. *20*

Marris, P. and Rein, M. (1974) *Dilemmas of Social Reform.* Harmondsworth: Penguin. *29, 30, 33*

Martin, D. V. (1962) *Adventures in Psychiatry* Oxford: Cassirer. *18*

Maslow, A. H. (1962) *Toward a Psychology of Being* (2nd ed., enlarged, 1968). New York: Nostrand. *27*

Meehl, P. E. (1954) *Clinical Versus Statistical Prediction*. Minneapolis: University of Minnesota Press. *21*

Merton, R. K. (1967) *Social Theory and Social Structure*. New York: Free Press. *129*

Merton, R. K. (1973) *The Sociology of Science*. Chicago: The University of Chicago Press. *130*

Mowrer, O. H. and Mowrer, W. M. (1938) Enuresis – a method for its study and treatment. *American Journal of Orthopsychiatry* 8: 436–59. *58*

Ohlin, L. E., Coates, R. B. and Miller, A. D. (1974) Radical correctional reform: a case study of the Massachusetts Youth Correctional System. *Harvard Educational Review* 44: 74–111. *100*

Parkes, C. M. (1971). Psycho-social transitions: a field for study. *Social Science and Medicine* 5: 101–15. *94*

Parkes, C. M. (1975) *Bereavement*. Harmondsworth: Penguin. *91–2*

Pearl, A. and Reissman, F. (1965) *New Careers for the Poor*. New York: The Free Press; London: Macmillan. *36*

Pizzey, E. (1974) *Scream Quietly or the Neighbours Will Hear*. Harmondsworth: Penguin. *120*

Piven, F. F. and Cloward, R. A. (1972) *Regulating the Poor*. London: Tavistock. *30, 33*

Poser, E. G. (1966) The effectiveness of therapists' training on group therapeutic outcome. *Journal of Consulting Psychology* 30: 283–9 *34*

Reiff, R. (1966) Mental health manpower and institutional change. *American Psychologist* 21: 540–8. *119*

Rogers, C. R. (1961) *On Becoming a Person*. Boston: Houghton Mifflin; London: Constable. *27*

Rosenhan, D. L. (1973) On being sane in insane places. *Science 179*: 250–8; heated replies: 180, 356 ff. *130*

Rosenthal, D. and Kety, S. S. (eds) (1968) *The Transmission of Schizophrenia*. Oxford: Pergamon. *16*

Rutter, M. (1972) *Maternal Deprivation Reassessed*. Harmondsworth: Penguin. *90*

Ryan, W. (ed.) (1969) *Distress in the City*. Cleveland: The Press of Case Western Reserve University. *21–2, 35*

Rycroft, C. (ed.) (1966) *Psychoanalysis Observed*. London: Constable. *20*

Sarason, S. B. (1967) Toward a psychology of change and innovation. *American Psychologist* 22: 227–33. *12, 127*

Sarason, S. B., Levine, M., Goldenberg, I., Cherlin, D. and Bennett, E. (1966) *Psychology in Community Settings*. New York: Wiley. *12, 35, 97*

Scheff, T. J. (1966) *Being Mentally Ill*. London: Weidenfeld & Nicolson. *33*

Schein, E. H. (1965) *Organisational Psychology*. Englewood Cliffs, N.J.: Prentice-Hall. *33*

Shakow, D. (1969) *Clinical Psychology as Science and Profession*. Chicago: Aldine. *15*

Sheperd, M., Oppenheim, B. and Mitchell, S. (1971) *Childhood Behaviour and Mental Health*. London: University of London Press. *20*

Smith, M. B. and Hobbs, N. (1966) The community and the community mental health centres. *American Psychologist* 21: 499–509. *29*

Spielberger, C. D. (ed.) (1970) *Current Topics in Clinical and Community Psychology, Vol. 2*. New York: Academic Press. *33*

Stanton, A. H. and Schwartz, M. S. (1954) *The Mental Hospital.* New York: Basic Books. *24*

Stevens, B. C. (1973) Role of fluphenazine decanoate in lessening the burden of chronic schizophrenics on the community. *Psychological Medicine 3*: 141–58. *19*

Sullivan, H. S. (1953) *The Interpersonal Theory of Psychiatry.* New York: Norton. *22*

Susser, M. (1968) *Community Psychiatry.* New York: Random House. *24*

Szasz, T. S. (1962) *The Myth of Mental Illness.* London: Secker & Warburg. *16, 27, 33*

Tharp, R. G. and Wetzel, R. J. (1969) *Behaviour Modification in the Natural Environment.* New York: Academic. *58, 75*

Tizard, J. (1964) *Community Services for the Mentally Handicapped.* Oxford: Oxford University Press. *82*

Tizard, J. (1972) Research into services for the mentally handicapped: science and policy issues. *British Journal of Mental Subnormality 18*: 1–12. *80*

Tizard, J. (1973) Maladjusted children and the child guidance service. *London Education Review 2*: 22–37. *82, 88*

Tizard, J. and Grad, J. C. (1961) *The Mentally Handicapped and Their Families.* Oxford: Oxford University Press. *78*

Tizard, J., Rutter, M. and Whitmore, K. (1970) *Education, Health and Behaviour.* London: Longman. *82*

Torrie, M. (1970) *Begin Again.* London: Dent. *92*

Truax, C. B. and Carkhuff, R. R. (1967) *Toward Effective Counselling and Psychotherapy.* Chicago: Aldine. *20, 130*

Weiner, R. (1973) Twentieth century middle class colonisers. *Social Work Today 4*: 42–4. *33*

Wing, J. K. and Brown, G. W. (1970) *Institutionalism and Schizophrenia.* Cambridge: Cambridge University Press. *17, 132*

Young, M. and Willmott, P. (1957) *Family and Kinship in East London.* London: Routledge and Kegan Paul (Penguin, 1962). *11, 79*

Subject Index

144